QUICK COURSE®

in

MICROSOFT®

Word

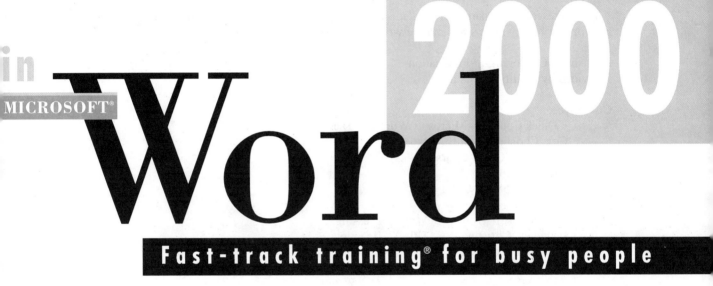

2000

Fast-track training® for busy people

JOYCE COX

CHRISTINA DUDLEY

PUBLISHED BY
Online Press
15442 Bel-Red Road
Redmond, WA 98052
Phone: (425) 885-1441, (800) 854-3344
Fax: (425) 881-1642
E-mail: quickcourse@otsiweb.com
Web site: www.quickcourse.com

Publisher's Cataloging-in-Publication
(Provided by Quality Books Inc.)

Cox, Joyce.
     Quick Course in Microsoft Word 2000 / Joyce
Cox, Christina Dudley. -- 1st ed.
     p. cm. -- (Quick Course books)
     Includes index.
     ISBN: 1-58278-002-1

     1. Microsoft Word.   2. Word processing.
I. Dudley, Christina.   II. Title.   III. Title:
Microsoft Word 2000   IV. Series.

Z52.5.M52C69 1999   652.5'5369
               QBI99-500179
                    99-070316
                    CIP

Printed and bound in the United States of America.

1 2 3 4 5 6 7 8 9 IPIP 3 2 1 0

Content overview

Content details

PART ONE: LEARNING THE BASICS

PART TWO: BUILDING PROFICIENCY

PART ONE

LEARNING THE BASICS

In Part One, we introduce the basic components of Microsoft Word and show you how to create and work with simple documents. In Chapter 1, you learn efficient techniques for using the program while creating a business letter. In Chapter 2, we cover editing techniques. In Chapter 3, you work with templates and wizards, and explore ways to add eye-catching details to your documents. Then we show you how to print your documents on paper as well as publish them on the Web. When you finish with Part One, you'll be ready to work with the majority of the documents you create in Word.

1

Getting Started

As you write a simple business letter, you learn techniques for creating and saving documents, giving instructions using the mouse and the keyboard, and applying formatting. Then we show you how to get help and quit Word.

The sample document for this chapter is a simple letter written in a straightforward style with classic formatting. You can easily adapt this letter to meet a variety of business and personal needs.

Document created and concepts covered:

Produce simple documents like this letter, right away

Adjust the top margin to make the document sit lower on the page

Vary the alignment to add interest and balance the page

Use bold and underlining for emphasis

July 1, 1999

Fern Leaf, President
ChillFill Inc.
3500 NW Bay Street
Juneau, AK 99801

RE: GLACIER SERIES SLEEPING BAG LAUNCH PARTY

Dear Fern:

I am pleased to announce that In The Bag's **Glacier Series**, our latest line of sleeping bags, is now complete and ready for production. Thanks to the hard work of our development team, the product was finished ahead of schedule. I want to thank your company for its contribution to the product. The use of ChillFill insulation is instrumental in making Glacier bags so unique and exciting. Many retail stores have already placed large orders for these innovative, subzero-temperature sleeping bags.

We're throwing a party on Saturday, August 21, 1999 to honor those who contributed to the development of this excellent line. I will contact you next week with further details. I hope you will be able to attend.

Again, thank you!

Al Pine

Justify paragraphs to give the letter a formal look

Microsoft Word 2000 is a powerful word-processing program that may seem daunting at first. That's why we start with the easy stuff! In this chapter, we show you how to save and retrieve documents, how to enter text and move around a document with reasonable efficiency, and how to select text so that you can do something with it. We cover all these topics while creating a short letter, and by the time you finish this chapter, you will know enough to create simple documents using Word.

We assume that you have installed Word 2000 on your computer and that you allowed the setup program to stash everything where it belongs on your C: drive. (If Word was installed on your computer by a network administrator, be sure to read the tip on the facing page.) We also assume that you have worked with Microsoft Windows before. If you are new to Windows, we recommend you take a look at *Quick Course®* in Microsoft Windows, another book in our series, which will help you come up to speed in no time at all.

Creating a New Document

Well, let's jump right in! Follow these steps to create your first Word document:

1. Click the Start button at the left end of the Windows taskbar.

2. On the Start menu, first click Programs and then click Microsoft Word.

3. If necessary, click the Office Assistant's Start Using Microsoft Word option. (We discuss the Office Assistant on page 27. As you follow along with our examples, the Office Assistant will entertain you with some cute antics and may display a message or a light bulb. Other than responding to messages, you can ignore it for now.) Your screen now looks like the one shown at the top of the facing page. (You'll learn what all the labeled parts of the window are as you work your way through this chapter.)

Other ways to start Word

Instead of starting Word by choosing it from the Start menu, you can create a shortcut icon for Word on your desktop. Right-click an open area of the desktop and choose New and then Shortcut from the shortcut menu. In the Create Shortcut dialog box, click the Browse button, navigate to the C:\Program Files\Microsoft Office\Office folder, and double-click Winword. Then click Next. Type a name for the shortcut icon and click Finish. For maximum efficiency, you can start Word and open a recently used document by choosing the document from the Documents submenu of the Start menu, where Windows stores the names of up to 15 of the most recently opened files. If you are using Microsoft Office 2000, you can also choose Open Office Document from the top of the Start menu and navigate to the folder in which the document you want to open is stored. To start Word and open a new document, you can choose New Office Document from the top of the Start menu and then double-click the Blank Document icon.

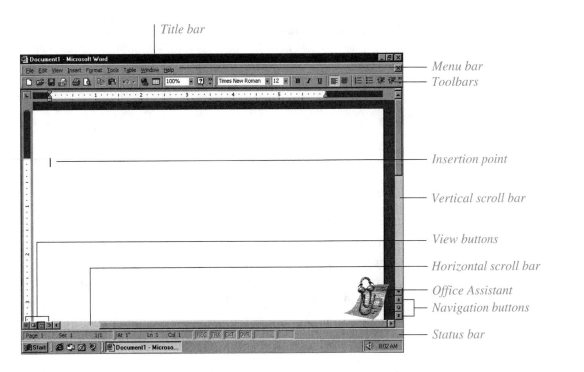

Title bar

Menu bar

Toolbars

Insertion point

Vertical scroll bar

View buttons

Horizontal scroll bar

Office Assistant

Navigation buttons

Status bar

To reduce screen clutter and display more of the document window, let's turn off the Windows taskbar.

Turning off the taskbar

1. Click the Start button, click Settings, and then click Taskbar & Start Menu (Windows 98) or Taskbar (Windows 95 and NT).

2. In the Taskbar Properties dialog box, click the Auto Hide check box to select it, then click OK, and finally click a blank area of the Word window to activate it. The taskbar disappears, and you'll notice that the Word window expands to fill up the newly available space.

3. Point to the bottom of the screen to make the taskbar temporarily reappear, and then move the pointer away from the bottom of the screen to hide the taskbar again.

Entering Text

Let's start by writing a paragraph. Follow these steps:

1. The blinking *insertion point* indicates where the next character you type will appear on the screen. Type the text shown on the following page.

Different configurations

We wrote this book using a computer running Microsoft Windows 98 with the screen resolution set to 800x600. If you are using a different version of Windows or a different resolution, the appearance of your screens won't match ours exactly. We also used the Word configuration that results when you do a Typical installation of Microsoft Office 2000 from CD-ROM. If a network administrator installed Word on your computer, your setup may be different. Don't be alarmed; you will still be able to follow along with most of the examples in this book.

I am pleased to announce that In The Bag's Glacier Series, our latest line of sleeping bags, is now complete and ready for production. Thanks to the hard work of our development team, the product was finished ahead of schedule. I want to thank your company for its contribution to the product. The use of ChillFill insulation is instrumental in making Glacier bags so unique and exciting. Many retail stores have already placed large orders for these innovative, subzero-temperature sleeping bags.

Word wrapping →

As each line of text reaches the right edge of the screen, the next word you type moves to a new line. This is called *word wrapping*. When entering text in Word, you don't have to worry about pressing the Enter key to end one line and start another. Word takes care of that chore for you, filling each line with as many words as will fit. (As you follow our examples, don't worry if your word wrapping isn't identical to ours.)

2. Press Enter to end the paragraph. Your screen looks like this:

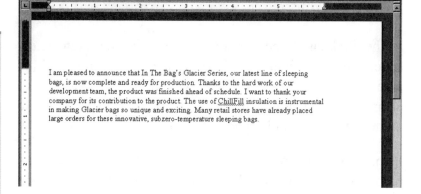

Correcting mistakes

Word corrects some simple typos, such as *teh* (the) and *adn* (and); we explain how on page 38. If you spell a less common word incorrectly—or if you use proper nouns or other correct but obscure spellings—Word points out the mistake with a red, wavy underline. (We explain why on page 52.) If Word thinks you've made a grammatical mistake, it uses a green, wavy underline. We show you some editing techniques on page 24, but in the meantime, if you make a mistake and want to correct it, press the Backspace key until you've deleted the error and then retype the text.

With a little text on the screen, you now have something to work with. But first let's cover some navigation basics.

Moving Around

You need to know how to move around a document for two reasons: so that you can view a document that is too long to fit on the screen, and so that you can edit its text.

The document window is often not big enough to display all of its contents. To bring out-of-sight information into view, you use the vertical and horizontal scroll bars. Clicking the arrow at the end of a scroll bar moves the window's contents a small distance in the direction of the arrow. Clicking on either side of a scroll box (both of which are now at the ends of their scroll bars) moves the contents one windowful. The position of the scroll box in relation to the scroll bar indicates the position of the window in relation to its contents. Drag the scroll box to see specific parts of a document—for example, the middle or end. (As you move the vertical scroll box in a multi-page document, Word displays the corresponding page number in a box beside the scroll bar.)

Scrolling

When it comes to editing, the insertion point is where the action is. Clicking anywhere in the text on the screen moves the insertion point to that location, or you can move the insertion point with the navigation keys, like this:

Navigation keys

To move the insertion point...	Press...
One character left or right	Left Arrow or Right Arrow
One word left or right	Ctrl+Left Arrow or Ctrl+Right Arrow
One line up or down	Up or Down Arrow
One paragraph up or down	Ctrl+Up Arrow or Ctrl+Down Arrow
One screenful up or down	PageUp or PageDown
To left or right end of current line	Home or End
To first or last character in document	Ctrl+Home or Ctrl+End
To previous editing location	Shift+F5

(In this book, we indicate that two or more keys are to be pressed together by separating the key names with a plus sign. For example, *press Ctrl+Home* means hold down the Ctrl key while simultaneously pressing the Home key.)

Selecting Text

Before you can do much with this paragraph, we need to discuss how to select text. Knowing how to select text efficiently saves time because you can then edit or format all the selected text at once, instead of a letter or word at a time. The simplest way to learn how to select text is to actually do it, so follow these steps to select some text blocks:

1. Move the pointer to the word *finished* and double-click it. The word changes to white on black to indicate that it is selected (or *highlighted*), as shown here:

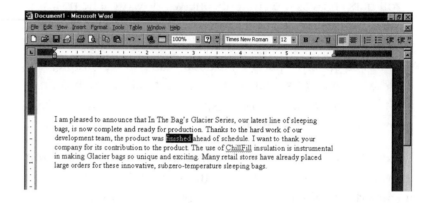

2. Point to the left of *ChillFill* and then click the left mouse button to position the insertion point at the beginning of the word. Next point to the right of *insulation*, hold down the Shift key, and click the left mouse button. (This action is called *Shift-clicking*.) Word highlights the words between the two clicks:

Shift-clicking →

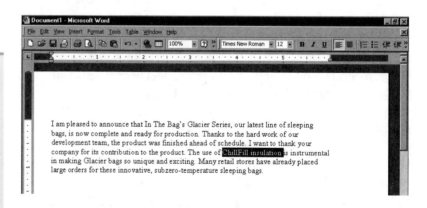

3. Point to the left of the word *innovative*, hold down the left mouse button, then drag to the right until *innovative, subzero-temperature sleeping bags* is selected, and release the mouse button. Using this technique, you can easily highlight exactly as much or as little text as you need.

Whole word selection

By default, Word selects whole words. For example, if you start a selection in the middle of a word and drag beyond the last character, Word selects the entire word. If you drag to the first character of the next word, Word selects that word, and so on. You can tell Word to select only the characters you drag across by choosing Options from the Tools menu, clicking the Edit tab, clicking the When Selecting Automatically Select Entire Word check box to deselect it, and clicking OK.

4. Click an insertion point to the left of the *T* in *Thanks*. Hold down the Shift key, press the Right Arrow key until the entire word is highlighted, and release the Shift key.

5. Without changing the selection, hold down the Shift key again, press the Down Arrow key, and then press the Left or Right Arrow key until the entire sentence is highlighted, like this:

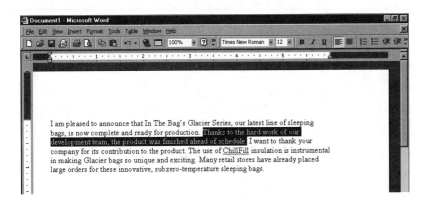

6. Next try pressing different Arrow keys while holding down the Shift key. As long as you hold down Shift, Word extends the selection in the direction of the key's arrow.

7. Release the Shift key and then press Home to move the insertion point to the beginning of the line where the selection starts. Moving the insertion point removes any highlighting.

8. Move the mouse pointer to the far left side of the window. When the pointer changes to an arrow, it is in an invisible vertical strip called the *selection bar*.

The selection bar

9. Still in the selection bar, point to the line containing *ChillFill* and click the left mouse button to highlight the line like this:

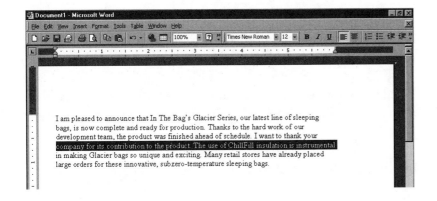

10. Now highlight the entire paragraph by double-clicking in the selection bar next to the paragraph. (If the Office Assistant displays a light bulb to indicate that it has a tip for you, ignore it for now. Or if you can't resist, click the light bulb, read the tip, and click OK.)

You can also drag the pointer in the selection bar to select multiple lines or paragraphs. To select all of the paragraphs in a document, you can triple-click in the selection bar.

Giving Instructions

Now that you know how to select text, let's discuss how you tell Word what to do with the selection. You give instructions by clicking buttons on toolbars, by choosing menu commands, and by pressing keyboard shortcuts.

Using the Toolbars

Word comes with many built-in toolbars, each equipped with buttons that are appropriate for a particular type of task. By default, Word displays two of its most useful toolbars—the Standard and Formatting toolbars—on a single toolbar row below the menu bar. It overlaps the toolbars and initially displays only the most frequently used buttons on each bar. As shown here, each toolbar has a move handle at its left end and a More Buttons button at its right end, both of which allow you to display currently hidden buttons:

The More Buttons button

Standard toolbar   *Move handle* *Formatting toolbar*

Move handles

More Buttons button   *More Buttons button*

Throughout this book we use toolbar buttons whenever possible because they are often the fastest way to access commands. Let's explore the toolbars:

1. Point to each button in turn, pausing until its name appears in a box below the pointer. This feature is called *ScreenTips*.

ScreenTips

2. Use any of the methods discussed on pages 8 and 9 to select the first occurrence of *Glacier Series*.

3. Click the Bold button on the Formatting toolbar.

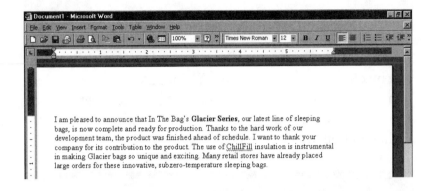

B

The Bold button

4. Press Home to remove the highlighting. As you can see, this simple change really makes the text stand out:

5. Select the first occurrence of *Glacier Series* again and notice that the Bold button appears "pressed." If a selection is already bold, clicking the pressed Bold button turns off bold formatting. This type of button is called a *toggle*, because it toggles a specific feature on and off.

Let's see how you can display more buttons on the Standard toolbar by displaying fewer buttons on the Formatting toolbar:

1. Point to the Formatting toolbar's move handle, and when the pointer changes to a four-headed arrow, drag it to the right until only the Font box and Bold button are visible, like this:

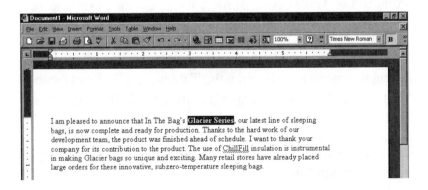

2. With the first occurrence of *Glacier Series* still selected, click the Formatting toolbar's More Buttons button to display a palette of all the hidden buttons on that toolbar, as shown on the next page.

I am pleased to announce that In The Bag's Glacier Series, our latest line of sleeping

The Underline and Italic buttons

3. Click the Underline button. (You could also add italic formatting by clicking the Italic button.) Word underlines the selection and adjusts the relative amount of space allocated to the two toolbars on the toolbar row so that it can display the Underline button, as shown here:

You can display and hide any toolbar at any time. You can also move, resize, and hide toolbars. Let's experiment with a different toolbar:

The Tables And Borders button

1. Click the Tables And Borders button. A floating Tables And Borders toolbar, with a title bar and a Close button, appears.

Docking a toolbar

2. Double-click the toolbar's title bar to "dock" it below the toolbar row. The docked toolbar's title bar disappears and it now has a move handle.

Moving a toolbar to the toolbar row

3. Point to the Tables And Borders toolbar's move handle and drag the toolbar up into the toolbar row so that it joins the overlapped Standard and Formatting toolbars.

4. Using the move handle, drag the Tables And Borders toolbar from the toolbar row over the document, where it becomes a floating toolbar again.

5. Point to the toolbar's title bar and drag all the way to the right side of the window. Just when you think the toolbar is going to disappear off the screen, it changes shape and docks itself along the right edge.

6. Experiment with moving the floating toolbar to various positions and docking and undocking it. (Notice that double-

clicking the floating toolbar's title bar docks the toolbar wherever it was last docked.)

7. Finally, click the Close button at the right end of the floating toolbar's title bar to remove the toolbar from the screen.

Now let's experiment with the document's font and font size:

1. Select the paragraph and click the arrow to the right of the Font box to display a list of the available fonts.

Changing the font

2. If necessary, use the scroll bar to bring the top of the list into view and then click Arial. The text's font changes, and the setting in the Font box now reflects this change.

3. With the paragraph still selected, click the Formatting toolbar's More Buttons button, click the arrow to the right of the Font Size box, and then click 11 in the drop-down list.

Changing the font size

4. Now press End so that you can see the results:

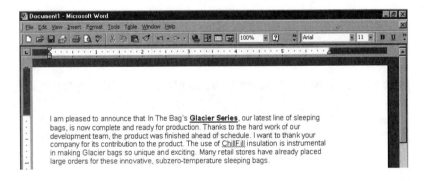

You have just used toolbar buttons and boxes to apply common character formats to a text selection. *Character formats* affect the appearance of individual characters. They can be applied to any number of characters, from one to the whole document. You can use toolbar buttons to change *paragraph formats*, which, as their name suggests, affect the appearance of an entire paragraph. Let's see how changing the alignment of a paragraph affects the way it looks:

Character formats

Paragraph formats

1. Press Ctrl+Home to move to the beginning of the document and then type the text shown on the following page. Press Enter to end paragraphs and create blank lines where indicated, and press Enter twice after the salutation.

July 1, 1999 (Press Enter twice)
Fern Leaf, President (Press Enter)
ChillFill Inc. (Press Enter)
3500 NW Bay Street (Press Enter)
Juneau, AK 99801 (Press Enter twice)
RE: GLACIER SERIES SLEEPING BAG LAUNCH PARTY
(Press Enter twice)
Dear Fern: (Press Enter twice)

2. If the Office Assistant offers to help you write the letter, click Cancel to close its message box.

3. Press Crtl+Home, click the More Buttons button on the Formatting toolbar (shown earlier on page 10), and then click the Align Right button to right-align the date. (Notice that Word adds the Align Right button to the displayed buttons on the Formatting toolbar.)

The Align Right button

4. That doesn't look right, so click the Align Left button on the More Buttons palette to return the date to the left side.

The Align Left button

5. Click an insertion point anywhere in the subject (RE:) line and then click the Center button. Here are the results:

The Center button

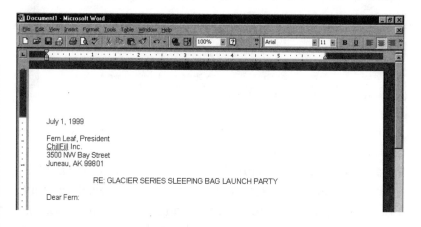

Click and type

When you know you want to center or right-align text, you can double-click to place an insertion point in the appropriate spot and then immediately start typing. For example, to quickly add a centered title, double-click in the middle of a page and then start typing. If double-clicking doesn't place the insertion point, choose Options from the Tools menu and select the Enable Click And Type check box. (This feature works only in print layout and web layout views.)

Using Menu Commands

Most of the buttons on the toolbars have equivalent commands on Word's menus, which are arranged on the menu bar that spans the window below the title bar. In addition, you can choose some commands from shortcut menus, which appear when you click elements of the document or the window using the right mouse button. We discuss both types of menus in this section.

So when do you use a button and when do you use a command? You can always use a command to carry out a particular task, but you can't always use a corresponding button. Clicking the button carries out its associated command with its default (predefined) settings without any further input from you. If a command is not represented by a toolbar button or if you want to use a command with something other than its default settings, you need to choose the command from a menu.

Buttons vs. commands

Choosing Menu Bar Commands

Because the procedure for choosing menu commands is the same for all Windows applications, we assume that you are familiar with it. Here's a quick review:

- To choose a command from a menu, you first click the menu name on the menu bar. When the menu drops down, you simply click the name of the command you want.

- To choose a command with the keyboard, you press the Alt key to activate the menu bar, press the underlined letter of the name of the menu, locate the command you want, and then press its underlined letter.

- To close a menu without choosing a command, you click away from the menu or press Esc once to close the menu and then again to deactivate the menu bar.

- Some command names are followed by an arrowhead, indicating that a *submenu* will appear when you choose that command. You choose commands from submenus as you would from regular menus.

Submenus

- Some command names are followed by an ellipsis (...), indicating that you must supply more information before Word can carry out the command. When you choose one of these commands, Word displays a *dialog box*. Some dialog boxes have several sheets called *tabs*. You can display the options on a tab by clicking it. You give the information needed to carry out a command by typing in an *edit box* or by selecting

Dialog boxes

options from *lists* and clicking *check boxes* and *option buttons*. You close the dialog box and carry out the command according to your specifications by simply clicking a command button (usually OK or Close) or by clicking the Close button in the top right corner. Clicking Cancel closes the dialog box and cancels the command. Other command buttons might be available to open other dialog boxes or to refine the original command.

● Some command names are occasionally displayed in gray letters, indicating that you can't choose them. For example, the Paste command is not available until you have cut or copied a selection.

Word 2000 goes beyond these basics by determining which commands you will most likely use and adjusting the display of commands on each menu to reflect how you use the program. As a quick example, we'll run through the steps for choosing a command and do some useful exploring at the same time. Follow these steps:

Short menus

1. Click *View* on the menu bar to drop down the View menu. Two arrows at the bottom of the menu indicate that one or more commands are hidden because they are not ones most people use frequently.

Expanded menus

2. Continue pointing to the word *View*. The two arrows disappear and the remaining commands on the menu appear, as shown here:

View
Normal
Web Layout
Print Layout
Outline
Toolbars ▶
✓ Ruler
Document Map
Header and Footer
Footnotes
Comments
Full Screen
Zoom...

Corresponding buttons

You might notice that for some menu commands, an icon appears to the left of the command name. The icon simply indicates that a corresponding button exists for this command on one of Word's toolbars. In the case of the four commands at the top of the View menu, the buttons appear at the left end of the horizontal scroll bar.

The View menu provides commands for customizing the screen display. Notice that the status of the less frequently used commands is indicated by a lighter shade.

3. Choose the Full Screen command by clicking it. The workspace containing your document expands to fill the entire screen, like this:

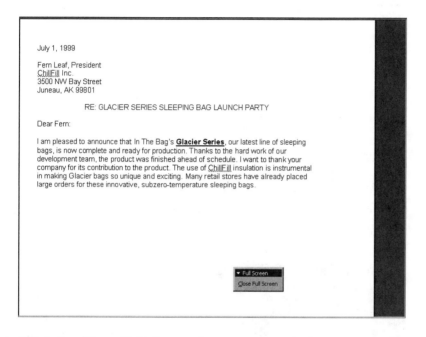

July 1, 1999

Fern Leaf, President
ChillFill Inc.
3500 NW Bay Street
Juneau, AK 99801

RE: GLACIER SERIES SLEEPING BAG LAUNCH PARTY

Dear Fern:

I am pleased to announce that In The Bag's **Glacier Series**, our latest line of sleeping bags, is now complete and ready for production. Thanks to the hard work of our development team, the product was finished ahead of schedule. I want to thank your company for its contribution to the product. The use of ChillFill insulation is instrumental in making Glacier bags so unique and exciting. Many retail stores have already placed large orders for these innovative, subzero-temperature sleeping bags.

▼ Full Screen
Close Full Screen

4. Click the Close Full Screen button to return the screen to its regular display, and then click *View* on the menu bar again. The Full Screen command is no longer hidden and appears in the same color as other frequently used commands.

5. Turn off the rulers by choosing Ruler from the expanded View menu. Word hides the rulers located below the toolbars and on the left side of the document window.

6. Choose Ruler from the View menu to redisplay the rulers. (If your rulers were already turned off, choosing Ruler the first time turns them on and choosing the command a second time turns them back off.)

7. Click the View menu again and point to Toolbars to display the submenu shown at the top of the next page.

Reappearing ruler

When the rulers are turned off, you can temporarily view the top ruler by pointing to the gray bar below the toolbars. The ruler drops down and remains visible as long as the pointer is over it. When you move the pointer away from it, the ruler disappears. Similarly, you can display the left ruler by pointing to the gray bar on the left side of the screen.

You can turn a toolbar on or off by choosing it here, but instead, let's look at another way to turn toolbars on or off.

8. Choose Customize from the Toolbars submenu and if necessary, click the Toolbars tab to display this dialog box:

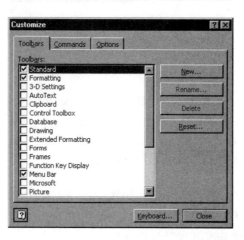

On the Toolbars tab, you can turn several toolbars on or off at one time by clicking their check boxes and then clicking the Close button. You can also customize your toolbars (see Word's Help feature for more information).

9. Click Close to close the dialog box.

Choosing Shortcut Menu Commands

For efficiency, the commands you are likely to use with a particular object, such as a block of text, are combined on special menus, called *shortcut menus*. Shortcut menus are also available for window elements, such as the toolbars. You access a shortcut menu by pointing to the object and then clicking the right mouse button. This is called *right-clicking*. Try the following:

1. Point to one of the toolbars and right-click to display the toolbar shortcut menu, which looks very similar to the Toolbars submenu shown on the facing page. (You can turn a toolbar on or off by choosing it from this shortcut menu.)

2. Right-click the Office Assistant and choose Hide from the shortcut menu to temporarily turn off the Office Assistant.

◄—— Shortcut menus

◄—— Right-clicking

◄—— Another way to display toolbars

◄—— Hiding the Office Assistant

Using Keyboard Shortcuts

We can't imagine anyone wanting to work with Word using only the keyboard. Using a mouse makes working with most Windows applications much easier, and Word is no exception. However, if your hands are already on the keyboard, using keyboard shortcuts to access commands can be more efficient. You have already used the Ctrl+Home shortcut to move to the top of the document. Here are a few more examples:

1. Select the subject line (*RE: GLACIER SERIES SLEEPING BAG LAUNCH PARTY*) and press first Ctrl+B and then Ctrl+U to make the line bold and underlined. (As you know, you can achieve the same effect by clicking the Bold and Underline buttons on the Formatting toolbar.)

2. Now use a keyboard shortcut to change the alignment of the main paragraph. Click an insertion point in the paragraph that begins *I am pleased* and press Ctrl+J to justify it so that its lines are even with both the left and right margins. (Pressing Ctrl+L would left-align the paragraph, Ctrl+R would right-align it, and Ctrl+E would center it.)

3. Press Ctrl+Home to move the insertion point to the top of the document. The results are shown on the next page.

Help with shortcuts

The list of keyboard shortcuts is extensive, and it would take a lot of space to reproduce it here. For more information about keyboard shortcuts, ask the Office Assistant or use the Index tab to search for "shortcut keys." (See page 27 for more information about the Help system.)

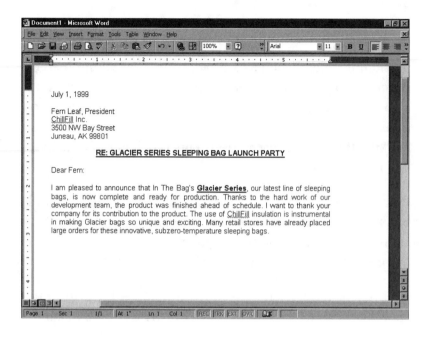

Saving Documents

Until you save the document you have created as a file on a disk, the document exists only in the computer's memory and disappears if the computer is intentionally or unintentionally turned off. To save the document for the first time, you can click the Save button or choose Save As from the File menu to display a dialog box in which you specify a name for the document. Let's save the document now on the screen:

Saving elsewhere

To store a file in a folder other than My Documents, click the arrow to the right of the Save In box, use the drop-down list to find the folder you want, and double-click it to open it. You can also use the icons on the shortcuts bar to access common folders and recently used files. To make a new folder, click the Create New Folder button. To change the default folder, choose Options from the Tools menu, click the File Locations tab, click Modify, and specify a new location.

Saving options

When saving a document, you can change the file format by clicking the arrow to the right of the Save As Type edit box in the Save As dialog box and then selecting a format. Clicking the Tools button displays a list of things you can do with the selected file; select General Options to display more choices. If you select Always Create Backup Copy, Word creates a copy of an existing document before overwriting it with a new version, naming the copy Backup of *Filename*. By default, the Allow Background Saves and Save AutoRecover Info Every options are turned on. You can turn them off or change the amount of time between background saves. If you assign a password in the Password To Open edit box in the File Sharing Options section, Word won't open this document until the password is entered correctly. If you assign a password in the Password To Modify edit box, Word opens a read-only version of the document if the password is *not* entered correctly; the read-only version can be altered, but it must be saved with a different name.

1. Choose Save As from the File menu to display the Save As dialog box:

Save As

Save in:	My Documents
History	
My Documents	
Desktop	
Favorites	
Web Folders	File name: July 1 — Save
	Save as type: Word Document — Cancel

2. Word suggests *July 1,* the first "phrase" in the document, as the filename. With *July 1* highlighted, type *ChillFill Letter* in the File Name edit box. (Word can handle long filenames, meaning that the filenames can have up to 255 characters, and they can contain spaces. They cannot contain the < > : * | \ " " ? and / characters.)

Filename specifications

3. Click Save to save the document in the My Documents folder on your hard drive.

From now on, you can click the Save button any time you want to save changes to this document. Because Word knows the name of the document, it simply saves the file by overwriting the old version with the new version.

The Save button

More Ways to Create New Documents

Part of the magic of a computer is that you can use the same information for different purposes without retyping the information each time. When you have already created one document and you want to adapt it for a different purpose without destroying the original, you can create a copy by saving the document with a new name. The original document remains unaltered under its own filename. Try this:

1. Choose Save As from the File menu.

2. Replace the name in the File Name edit box by typing *Launch Party Letter*, and click Save. Word creates a copy of the file, closes the original letter, and changes the name in the title bar to Launch Party Letter.

You can create a totally new document at any time without closing any open documents. Follow these steps:

The New button

1. Click the New button on the Standard toolbar. Word displays a new document called Document2, completely obscuring Launch Party Letter, which is still open.

2. Type the following paragraph, misspelling *Saturday* and *honor* (Word will underline them with red, wavy lines):

*We're throwing a party on **Saterday**, August 21, 1999 to **honur** those who contributed to the development of this excellent line. I hope that you will be able to attend. I will contact you with more details next week.*

3. Press Enter and then save the document with the name *Glacier Bag Party*.

Opening Documents

You now have a couple of open documents in separate, stacked windows. For good measure, let's open an existing document:

The Open button

1. Click the Open button on the Standard toolbar to display the dialog box shown here:

2. With ChillFill Letter selected, click Open.

Manipulating Windows

We'll pause here to review some window basics:

1. Display the Windows taskbar and click the Launch Party Letter button to activate that document. ◄——————

Activating documents
from the taskbar

2. Choose Arrange All from the expanded Window menu. Now the three open documents each occupy a third of the screen: ◄——————

Arranging windows

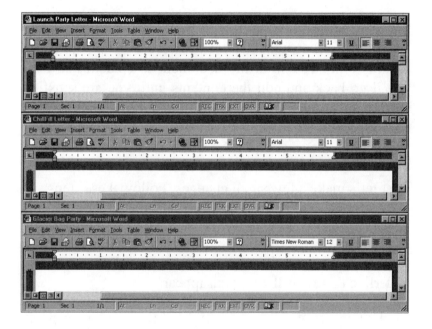

Finding files

Suppose you can't remember what you called a document or where you stored it. In the Open dialog box, click the Tools button, click Find, enter the appropriate drive in the Look In box, click the Search Subfolders check box, and check that File Name is selected in the Property edit box. Select the appropriate option in the Condition edit box and then enter any part of the filename you remember in the Value edit box. Click Add To List to add your criteria to the criteria list and then click Find Now. Word searches this drive and its subfolders for any Word documents with the Value entry in their filenames and lists the ones it finds. You can then select the document you want and click Open. If you have many documents with similar names, refine the search by specifying other properties such as text in the document or its date of modification. To save searches, click the Save Search button, name the search, and click OK.

Managing files

To print, delete, rename, or move a document from Word's Open dialog box, simply right-click its filename in the Open dialog box and choose a command from the shortcut menu. You can perform most of these tasks from the Save As dialog box as well. (You can also click the Tools button on the dialog box's toolbar to drop down a file-management menu.)

Notice that the title bar of the active window is a different color than those of the inactive windows. Any entries you make and most commands you choose will affect only the document in the active window.

Maximizing a window

3. Click anywhere in Glacier Bag Party to activate it, then click the Glacier Bag Party window's Maximize button (the middle of the three buttons at the right end of the window's title bar). The window expands to fill the screen, completely obscuring Launch Party Letter and ChillFill Letter.

Simple Editing

When creating documents, you will usually start by typing roughly what you want the document to contain and then you'll go back and edit the contents until you are satisfied with them. In this section, we'll quickly cover some basic editing techniques.

Deleting and Replacing Text

First let's make a few small changes. Follow these steps:

1. Click an insertion point to the left of the *e* in *Saterday*, press the Delete (Del) key to delete the character to the right, and without moving the insertion point, type *u*. The red, wavy underline that flags the typo disappears.

2. Click an insertion point to the right of the *u* in *honur*, press Backspace to delete the character to the left, and type *o*.

3. Select the word *that* in the second line, and press either Delete or Backspace to delete the word.

4. Double-click the word *more* in the third line and, with the word highlighted, type *further* as its replacement.

5. Click the Save button to save Glacier Bag Party.

Moving and Copying Text

You can move or copy any amount of text within the same document or to a different document. Move operations can be carried out using the Cut and Paste buttons on the Standard toolbar. Similarly, copy operations can be carried out using the Copy and Paste buttons. Let's experiment:

1. In Glacier Bag Party, select the words *next week* and click the Cut button on the Standard toolbar. Word removes the text from the document and stores it in a temporary storage place, called the *Clipboard*, in your computer's memory.

The Cut button

2. Click an insertion point to the left of the *w* in *with* and click the Paste button. Word inserts the cut text, preceding it with a space.

The Paste button

3. Select the sentence that begins *I hope you* and click the Cut button. (If the Clipboard toolbar appears, click its Close button and read the tip below.) Click an insertion point to the right of the last period in the text, and click the Paste button.

Now let's try copying text to a different document:

1. Choose Select All from the Edit menu to select all the text in Glacier Bag Party and then click the Copy button.

The Copy button

2. Choose Launch Party Letter from the Window menu or click its button on the taskbar to activate the letter.

3. Maximize the window and press Ctrl+End to move to the end of the letter. Press Enter to add a blank line and then click the Paste button to insert the selected paragraph.

When you copied the paragraph from Glacier Bag Party to Launch Party Letter, you copied the formatting of the paragraph as well. You'll reformat the entire letter in a moment.

The Office Clipboard

If you want to cut or copy several different items from one document and paste them into another, you can do so easily with the Office Clipboard. Unlike the Windows Clipboard, which holds only one item at a time, the Office Clipboard can hold up to 12 items from any Windows application. To use the Office Clipboard, first select an item, click the Cut or Copy button, and then select and cut or copy another item. The Clipboard toolbar appears on your screen. Each item you have cut or copied is represented by an icon of the program in which it was created. Point to any icon to have ScreenTips display its contents. You can paste up to 12 items at a time into any Office program. To paste one item, click an insertion point in the appropriate area and then click the icon that represents the item you want to paste. To paste all of the items at once, click the Paste All button on the Clipboard toolbar. To clear the items, click the Clear Clipboard button. To turn off the toolbar, click its Close button.

Undoing and Redoing Commands

For those occasions when you make an editing mistake, Word provides a safety net: the Undo command. Try this:

The Undo button

1. You're not sure you need the paragraph you copied into the letter, so click the Undo button to reverse the paste operation from the previous steps.

The Redo button

2. You change your mind again, so click the Redo button to paste the paragraph back into the letter.

Before we show you how to get help, let's finish off the letter:

1. With the insertion point at the end of the letter, type *Again, thank you!*, press Enter four times, type *Al Pine*, and then press Enter again.

2. Choose Select All from the Edit menu and change the Font setting on the Formatting toolbar to Times New Roman and the Font Size setting to 10.

The Justify button

3. Finally, select the second paragraph, click the Formatting toolbar's More Buttons button, and click the Justify button.

4. Press Ctrl+Home. Then save the letter, which looks like this:

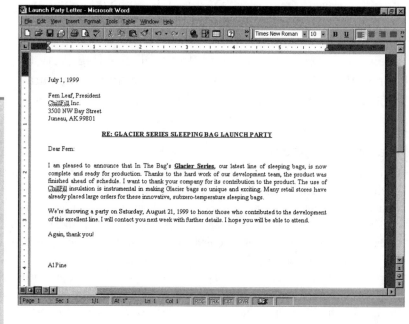

Undoing and redoing multiple actions

In Word, you can undo and redo several actions at a time. Click the arrow to the right of the appropriate button and drag through the actions in the list that you want to undo or redo. You cannot undo or redo a single action other than the last one. For example, to undo the third action in the list, you must also undo the first and second.

Getting Help

Are you worried that you might not remember everything
we've covered so far? Don't be. If you forget how to carry out
a particular task, help is never far away. You've already seen
how the ScreenTips feature can jog your memory about the
functions of the toolbar buttons. And you may have noticed
that the dialog boxes contain a Help button—the ? in the top ◄───── Help with dialog boxes
right corner—you can click to get information about their op-
tions. Here, you'll look at ways to get information using the
Office Assistant. Follow these steps:

1. Click the Microsoft Word Help button on the Standard tool- ◄───── The Microsoft Word Help
   bar. The Office Assistant appears with a box where you can   button
   type a question, as shown below:

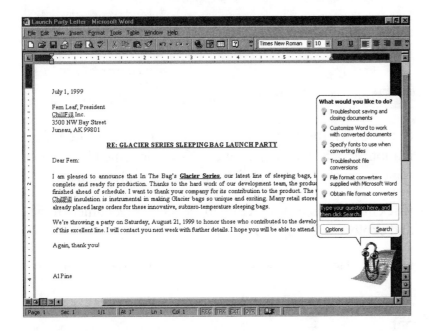

   If the Office Assistant is already visible, you can simply click
   the Assistant to display the box.

2. Sometimes the options in the box relate to the task you just
   completed, but in this case, click the search box, type *save*,
   and then click the Search button.

3. The Office Assistant offers several options to choose from. Click the Save A Document option to open the Help window on the right side of the screen as shown below. (It may take a few seconds for the help file to be prepared for use.)

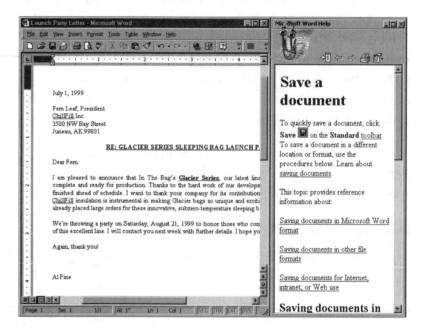

4. Scroll down the Help window, reading through the information, and then click the Save A New, Unnamed Document topic to display instructions on how to complete the task.

5. Click the Back button to return to the Save A Document topic, and explore other options.

6. Click the Help window's Close button to close the window.

More about the Office Assistant

If the Office Assistant displays a light bulb above its icon, it has a tip for you. Click the light bulb to see the tip. To move the Office Assistant to another place on the screen, drag it. You can display the search box by clicking the Office Assistant. If having the Office Assistant on the screen bothers you or if you would like to customize it, you can click the Office Assistant's Options button to open the Office Assistant dialog box. Here you can select and deselect various options that control when the Office Assistant appears, whether it makes sounds, and what tips it displays. To turn off the Office Assistant, deselect the Use The Office Assistant check box. (To make the Office Assistant temporarily disappear or reappear, choose Hide/Show The Office Assistant from the Help menu.) On the Gallery tab, you can click the Back or Next buttons to scroll through the animated characters available for the assistant (the default is the paper clip) and then click OK to change the assistant. (You may need to insert the installation CD-ROM to complete the switch.)

You can also search for specific information via the Help window. Follow these steps:

1. Choose Microsoft Word Help from the Help menu and then click one of the Office Assistant's help topics to redisplay the Help window.

2. Click the Show button to expand the Help window so that it shows the Contents, Answer Wizard, and Index tabs. (If necessary, drag the Office Assistant out of the way.)

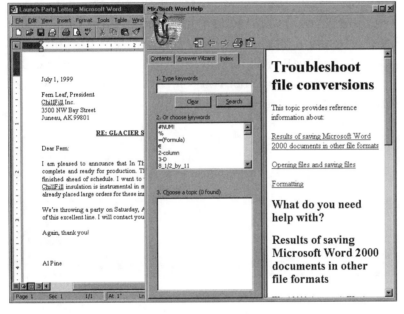

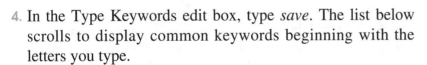

The Show button

Searching the Help Index

3. Click the Index tab to display these options:

4. In the Type Keywords edit box, type *save*. The list below scrolls to display common keywords beginning with the letters you type.

5. Click the Search button to display a list of topics that contain the word *save*.

6. In the Choose A Topic list, click Save A Document. Help redisplays the topic shown on the facing page.

7. Close the Help window.

We'll leave you to explore other Help topics of interest on your own.

Initial capital letters

Sometimes the capitalization we use doesn't exactly match what's on the screen. We capitalize the first letter of every word so that the words stand out in a sentence. For example, in the adjacent steps, we tell you to type in the Type Keywords edit box, when the name of the box on the screen is Type keywords.

Quitting Word

Well, that's it for the basic Word tour. We'll finish up by first showing you several ways to close a document and then how to quit Word:

Closing documents

1. On the Windows taskbar, right-click the ChillFill Letter document button and then choose Close from the shortcut menu to close the document.

2. To close the Launch Party Letter document, choose Close from the File menu.

3. To close Glacier Bag Party, press Alt, then F (the underlined letter in *File* on the menu bar), and then press C (the underlined letter in *Close* on the File menu). Because you have made changes to this document since you last saved it, the Office Assistant asks whether you want to save your changes before closing the document, like this:

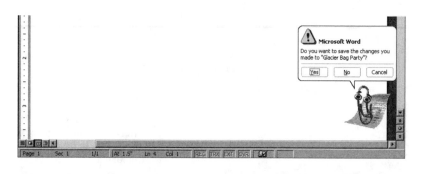

Using Contents

The Contents tab of the Help window displays various topics represented by book icons and their subtopics represented by question mark icons. To display a topic's subtopics, click the plus sign to the left of the book icon. When you find the subtopic you're looking for, click it. Help displays the information in the right pane.

Using Answer Wizard

The Answer Wizard provides a way to type search questions without the Office Assistant interface. To access the Answer Wizard, display the Help window, click the Answer Wizard tab, type a question in the edit box, and then click Search. Word then displays a list of topics that most closely fit your question. Double-click one of the topics to display its contents in the Help window's right pane.

Using the Web

If you have a modem and are connected to the Internet, you can access the Microsoft Office Update Web site as well as other Microsoft Web sites to get information or technical support. Choose Office On The Web from the Help menu to start your Web browser, connect to the Internet, and display the Microsoft Office Update Web site.

If the Office Assistant is not visible, this message appears in a dialog box, instead.

4. Click Yes.

5. To quit Word, click the Close button at the right end of the title bar.

Closing Word

Here are some other ways to quit Word:

- Choose Exit from the File menu.

- Press Alt, then F, and then X (the underlined letter in *Exit* on the File menu).

- Double-click the Control menu icon—the W—at the left end of Word's title bar.

Well, we've covered a lot of ground and you are now familiar with some of Word's basic elements. As you work your way through the rest of this book, you'll build on your Word skills while learning more complex techniques for word processing your documents.

Letter-Perfect Documents

You produce a longer document as you learn how to use the AutoText and AutoCorrect features. Then you explore more editing techniques and organize the document in outline view. Finally, you search for and replace text, and you check spelling and grammar.

Here you create a Frequently Asked Questions page, or FAQ. You can use FAQs, which answer the who-what-where about an organization, to introduce any company or group to potential customers or members.

Document created and concepts covered:

Assign heading levels and reorganize your documents in outline view

Glacier Sleeping Bags—Frequently Asked Questions

What is the Glacier Series of sleeping bags?

The Glacier Series was created for use in extreme weather conditions. Glacier sleeping bags are ideal for conditions ranging from 20 degrees Fahrenheit to –30 degrees Fahrenheit. Constructed with quality, rugged materials, Glacier sleeping bags meet the needs of the avid hiker or climber.

Find and replace text to maintain consistency

Who makes Glacier sleeping bags?

The Glacier Series was designed and manufactured by In The Bag. Founded in 1986 by world-class mountaineer Al Pine, In The Bag has been producing sleeping bags made from high quality materials for twelve years. Al Pine, the current president of In The Bag, decided to start the company after developing mild hypothermia during a hiking trip in Denali National Park. Among other accolades, In The Bag received the 1997 Rainier Award in Outdoor Product Design for their zipperless Kodiak bags. In The Bag's primary goal is to provide sleeping bags that guarantee a safe, comfortable sleeping atmosphere for people who explore even the farthest corners of the globe.

Use AutoText and AutoCorrect for often-used text

How are they constructed?

All models of Glacier sleeping bags are made of a durable polyester outer shell that withstands the roughest conditions nature offers. The Glacier 1000 and Glacier 2000 are insulated with ChillFill, an innovative fill made of 100% natural fibers. The Glacier 3000, designed for the coldest weather conditions, uses CozyTec, a new form of insulation created by In The Bag that uses rubber fibers spun from recycled tires as its base. The quilted construction of all three Glacier models ensures that the fill stays evenly distributed for maximum comfort and warmth.

Where are the bags made?

All materials used in Glacier sleeping bags are made in the USA. The bags are assembled in our manufacturing plant in Anchorage, Alaska.

Check spelling to avoid embarrassing typos

Have the bags been tested in extreme conditions?

In The Bag tests their sleeping bags in their on-site labs and on actual expeditions. In the labs, test dummies are used in simulations of extreme weather conditions, including temperature, precipitation, and wind-chill factors.

How much do they cost?

Prices for Glacier sleeping bags range from $150 to $400. Customized bags cost slightly more. Bulk discounts are available.

How do I order?

You can purchase Glacier sleeping bags in one of three ways: 1. You can buy them at most outdoor equipment stores. 2. You can order them directly from In The Bag by calling (800) 555-2400 or by faxing us at (907) 555-1451. 3. You can e-mail your order (and/or any further inquiries) to us at custserve@bag.tld.

Delete, copy, and move text until it reads exactly right

With Word, you can apply fancy formats and add graphics and special effects to increase the impact of a document. But all the frills in the world won't compensate for bad phrasing, bad organization, or errors. That's why this chapter focuses on the Word tools that help you develop and refine the content of your documents. The example for this chapter is a *frequently asked questions* (FAQ) document about In The Bag's new sleeping-bag line. An FAQ is often sent in information packages about an organization and is usually included in commercial Web sites on the Internet.

First let's enter a few headings to establish the basic structure of the document:

1. Start Word by clicking the Start button and choosing Microsoft Word from the Programs submenu. If necessary, turn off the rulers by choosing Ruler from the View menu. That way, you'll have a bit more room to work.

2. If you want, choose Hide The Office Assistant from the Help menu. (If you find the Office Assistant helpful, you might want to leave it turned on. It won't get in the way.)

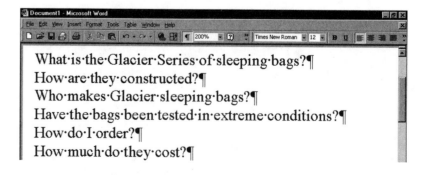

The Show/Hide ¶ button

3. Click the Standard toolbar's More Buttons button and then click the Show/Hide ¶ button to display nonprinting characters such as paragraph marks and spaces.

4. Type *What is the Glacier Series of sleeping bags?* and press Enter. Word enters the heading, inserts a paragraph mark, and moves the insertion point to the next line.

5. Type *How are they constructed?* and press Enter. Then continue entering the headings shown here. (We've magnified the document to make it easier to read.)

6. Now save the document by clicking the Save button, specifying *Frequently Asked Questions* as the name of the file, and clicking Save.

To get the ball rolling, let's add some text under a heading:

1. Click an insertion point between the question mark and the paragraph mark at the end of the *What is the Glacier Series of sleeping bags?* heading, press Enter, and then type the following text:

   The Glacier Series was created for use in extreme weather conditions. Glacier sleeping bags are ideal for conditions ranging from 20 degrees Fahrenheit to -30 degrees Fahrenheit. Constructed with quality, rugged materials, Glacier bags meet the needs of the avid hiker or climber.

You've typed *Glacier* three times. Let's look at a couple of ways you can save keystrokes and ensure that the words and phrases you use repeatedly are always entered correctly.

Storing and Retrieving Often-Used Text

To help you enter often-used text efficiently, accurately, and consistently, Word has two special features—AutoText and AutoCorrect. At first glance, these two features seem almost identical; they both enable you to store text or a graphic with a name and then insert the text or graphic in any document at any time simply by typing the name. An AutoText or Auto-Correct entry can be as short as a single text character or as long as several pages of text or graphics. Unlike the contents of the Windows Clipboard, AutoText and AutoCorrect entries are saved from one Word session to the next.

So what's the difference between them? To insert an AutoText entry, you type the entry's name and then press the F3 key. To insert an AutoCorrect entry, you simply type the name; the instant you type a punctuation mark or press the Spacebar, Word automatically replaces the name with its entry.

How do you decide which to use? Here's an example. Suppose you own a landscaping business. You know you'd save a lot of time and effort if you could type *aspen* instead of having to type and italicize *Populus tremuloides* (the botanical name

◄ AutoText vs. AutoCorrect

for the aspen tree) every time you include this tree in a materials list for your wholesaler. But when you communicate with your clients, you want to be able to refer to the aspen tree by its common name rather than its botanical name. This entry is a prime candidate for AutoText because you can control when Word replaces the name *aspen* with the entry *Populus tremuloides* and when it stays plain old *aspen*. If you use AutoCorrect instead, Word will always replace the name *aspen* with *Populus tremuloides*. Let's look at both features.

Using AutoText

You use Word's AutoText feature to store text or a graphic so that you can later retrieve it by typing its name and pressing the F3 key. For this example, you'll turn a word you have already typed into an AutoText entry. Follow these steps to simplify the typing of *Glacier*:

Displaying the AutoText toolbar

1. Right-click one of the toolbars and choose AutoText to display the AutoText toolbar.

2. Select *Glacier* in the sentence you just typed and click New on the AutoText toolbar to display this dialog box:

3. Type *g* in the Please Name Your AutoText Entry edit box and click OK. Word closes the dialog box.

Now let's use the entry you've just created as you write a few more paragraphs for the FAQ:

1. Click an insertion point after the question mark in the *How are they constructed?* paragraph, press Enter, and then type *All models of g* (don't press the Spacebar after *g*).

2. Press F3. Word replaces *g* with the *Glacier* entry.

3. Continue typing the following paragraph, using the *g-F3* sequence to insert *Glacier* where indicated. Be sure to type the

Formatted entries

If you want an AutoText or Auto-Correct entry to retain its paragraph formatting (alignment, indents, and so on), include the paragraph mark when you select the entry. AutoText entries retain their character formatting, but if you want an AutoCorrect entry to retain its character formatting, you must be sure to select the Formatted Text option on the AutoCorrect tab of the AutoCorrect dialog box when you create the entry.

error marked in bold exactly as you see it so that you will have a mistake to correct later in the chapter. (Word will flag this and any other spelling errors with a red, wavy underline.) Also include the **** characters, which are placeholders for information you'll add later.

bags are made of a durable **polester** *outer shell that withstands the roughest conditions nature offers. The g-F3 1000 and g-F3 2000 are insulated with ChillFill, an innovative fill made of 100% natural fibers. The g-F3 3000, designed for the coldest weather conditions, uses ****, a new form of insulation created by In The Bag that uses rubber fibers spun from **** as its base. The quilted construction of all three g-F3 models ensures that the fill stays evenly distributed for maximum comfort and warmth.*

Suppose you forget the code for an AutoText entry. Does that mean you can't use the entry anymore? Not at all. Try this:

1. Click an insertion point at the end of the *How much do they cost?* heading, press Enter, and then type *Prices for* followed by a space.

2. Click the AutoText button on the toolbar to display the Auto-Text tab of the AutoCorrect dialog box, shown here:

The AutoText button

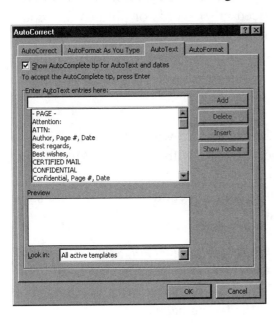

Deleting entries

To delete an AutoText entry, click the AutoText button, select the entry you want to delete from the list, click Delete, and then click OK. To delete an AutoCorrect entry, choose AutoCorrect from the Tools menu, select the entry you want to delete from the list found at the bottom of the AutoCorrect dialog box, click Delete, and then click OK.

3. Select *g* in the list of AutoText entries and then check the Preview box to see what the entry represents. (The list includes several ready-made entries, including AutoComplete entries; see the tip below.) To insert the selected entry, you could simply click the Insert button. Instead, click OK to close the dialog box, and we'll show you another way to insert the entry.

4. Click the All Entries button on the AutoText toolbar to display a drop-down list of categories of entries. Most of the categories pertain to writing a letter; the Normal category is where the entires you create are stored.

5. Point to each category in turn to see its contents.

6. Select Normal and then *g*. Word inserts the entry *Glacier* at the insertion point.

7. Finish typing the paragraph with this text:

   bags range from $150 to $400. Bulk discounts are available. Customized bags cost slightly more.

8. Turn off the AutoText toolbar by right-clicking it and selecting AutoText from the shortcut menu.

Now that you've simplified the typing of the word *Glacier*, you've probably noticed other words or phrases that could benefit from the same treatment. How about *In The Bag*? To simplify the typing of this entry, you'll use the AutoCorrect feature.

Using AutoCorrect

You use the AutoCorrect feature when you want Word to automatically replace a name with its entry. AutoCorrect names should be unique sequences of characters that you are not likely to use normally in a document. Follow these steps to get an idea of how this works:

1. In the paragraph that begins *All models of*, select *In The Bag* and then choose AutoCorrect from the expanded Tools menu to display the AutoCorrect tab of the AutoCorrect dialog box as shown at the top of the facing page.

AutoComplete

Some of the entries in the list on the AutoText tab of the Auto-Correct dialog box are entries for AutoComplete. All these "autos" may seem a bit confusing; put simply, after you type the first few characters of an AutoComplete entry, the entire entry appears. If it is correct, press Enter or F3 to insert the completed entry. If it is not correct, just ignore it and keep typing. AutoComplete finishes the date, days of the week, months, and your name, in addition to the AutoText entries in the list.

Word is waiting for you to enter the name you want Word to replace with the selected text, which appears in the With edit box. The box below contains a ready-made list of entries for symbols and commonly misspelled words, such as *teh* (the), which Word replaces each time you type them.

AutoCorrect's ready-made entries

2. In the Replace edit box, type *itb* as the name of the entry and click Add. Word adds the name and its replacement to the list. Then click OK to close the dialog box.

Now let's use this AutoCorrect entry so that you can get a feel for what a time-saver AutoCorrect can be:

1. Click an insertion point at the end of the *Have the bags been tested in extreme conditions?* heading, press Enter, and then type the following:

   itb tests their sleeping bags in their on-site labs and on actual expeditions. In the labs, test dummies are used in simulations of extreme weather conditions, including temperature, precipitation, and wind-chill factors.

2. Next click an insertion point at the end of the *How do I order?* heading, press Enter, and type the text shown on the next page. (Be sure to misspell *can* as *acn*, one of Word's ready-made AutoCorrect entries.)

Bypassing AutoCorrect

To turn off AutoCorrect, deselect the Replace Text As You Type check box on the AutoCorrect tab of the AutoCorrect dialog box. If you don't want to turn off Auto-Correct but you also don't want AutoCorrect to replace a particular instance of a name with its entry, type the name, and after AutoCorrect replaces it, click the Undo button.

You acn *purchase* g-F3 *bags in one of three ways: 1. You can buy them at most outdoor equipment stores. 2. You can order them directly from* itb *by calling (800) 555-2400 or by faxing us at (907) 555-1451. 3. You can e-mail your order (and/or any further inquiries) to us at custserve@bag.tld.*

3. Save the document. (Remember to save frequently in order to safeguard your work.)

More Editing Techniques

In Chapter 1, we covered some basic editing techniques that you may have already used in this chapter if you typed any words incorrectly. In this section, we briefly cover some more ways of revising documents. We'll make a few changes to the FAQ to get a feel for what's involved.

More Ways to Delete and Replace Text

Word provides a few techniques for deleting and replacing text in addition to those covered in Chapter 1. You'll learn these techniques as you add a new paragraph to the FAQ:

1. Click an insertion point at the end of the *Who makes Glacier sleeping bags?* heading and press Enter. Type the following (including the errors in bold and the AutoText and AutoCorrect names, which are not italicized):

The g-F3 *Series was designed and manufactured by* itb. *Founded in 1985 by world-class mountaineer Al Pine,* itb *has been producing outdoor sleeping bags made from high quality materials for twelve years. Al Pine,* teh **curunt** *president of* itb, *decided to start* teh *company after developing mild hypothermia during a hiking trip in Denali National Park. Among other accolades,* itb *received the 1997 Rainier Award in Outdoor Product Design for their innovative zipperless Kodiak bags.* itb*'s primary goal is to provide sleeping bags that guarantee a safe,* **comforatable** *sleeping atmosphere for people who explore even* teh *furthest corners of the globe.*

2. Click an insertion point to the right of the *r* in *outdoor* (in the second sentence) and then press Ctrl+Backspace to delete the word to the left of the insertion point.

3. Now click an insertion point to the left of the *i* in *innovative* and press Ctrl+Delete to delete the word to the right of the insertion point.

As you have seen, Word is by default in Insert mode. When you click an insertion point and begin typing, the characters you enter appear to the left of the insertion point, pushing any existing text to the right. Word can also operate in Overtype mode, so that when you click an insertion point and begin typing, each character you enter replaces an existing one.

Insert mode

Overtype mode

Let's experiment a bit with overtyping. Suppose In The Bag was actually founded in 1986, not 1985. Here's how to make this simple correction:

1. Click an insertion point between the *8* and *5* of *1985* under the *Who makes Glacier sleeping bags?* heading.

2. In the status bar, double-click the Overtype box (the third box from the right). The letters *OVR* are highlighted to indicate that you are now in Overtype mode.

3. Type *6*, which overtypes the 5, so that the entry now correctly reads *1986*.

4. Double-click the Overtype box to turn off Overtype mode. This step is important; you might overtype valuable information if you forget it.

More Ways to Move and Copy Text

As you saw in Chapter 1, you can move any amount of text within the same document or to a different document. Move operations can either be carried out using the Cut and Paste

Tracking editing changes

To keep track of editing changes, you can use tools available on the Reviewing toolbar. (Right-click a toolbar and choose Reviewing from the shortcut menu to display this toolbar.) Click the Track Changes button to display revisions underlined and in red. The letters *TRK* in the status bar indicate you are in track-changes mode. (To adjust the display of revisions, choose Options from the Tools menu and change the settings on the Track Changes tab.) You can insert comments using the Insert Comment button and save the document with comments using the Save Version button. To stop tracking changes, you can either click the Track Changes button on the Reviewing toolbar or double-click the letters *TRK* in the status bar.

Drag-and-drop editing →

buttons as discussed in Chapter 1 or using a mouse technique called *drag-and-drop editing*. Generally, you use drag-and-drop editing when moving text short distances—that is, when the text you're moving and its destination can be viewed simultaneously. Try this:

Moving text with
drag-and-drop editing →

1. Select the sentence that begins *Bulk discounts* under the *How much do they cost?* heading.

2. Point to the highlighted text, hold down the left mouse button, drag the shadow insertion point after the last period in the paragraph, and release the mouse button. The selected text moves to the specified location. You have, in effect, transposed the last two sentences in this paragraph.

3. Press End and if necessary, press Enter to add a new, blank paragraph at the end of the document.

4. Select the *How do I order?* heading and the following paragraph and then drag-and-drop them below the *How much do they cost?* heading and its paragraph.

The procedure for copying text is similar to that for moving text. Try copying some text with the drag-and-drop technique:

1. Press Ctrl+Home to move to the top of the document.

Copying text with
drag-and-drop editing →

2. Click an insertion point at the beginning of the sentence that reads *The Glacier Series* under the *Who makes Glacier sleeping bags?* heading.

No automatic replacement

You can have Word insert what you type to the left of a selection instead of replacing it. Choose Options from the Tools menu, and then click the Edit tab to display the editing options. Then simply click the Typing Replaces Selection check box to deselect it, and click OK.

Smart editing

When you cut or copy and paste text, Word guesses where spaces are needed in the text. For example, Word usually removes spaces before or adds spaces after punctuation marks. To instruct Word to leave these adjustments up to you, choose Options from the Tools menu, click the Edit tab, click the Use Smart Cut And Paste check box to deselect it, and click OK.

Drag-and-drop problems

If pointing to a text selection and then holding down the mouse button does not move the text but instead deselects the text and creates an insertion point, the Drag-And-Drop Text Editing option is turned off. To turn it on, choose Options from the Tools menu, click the Edit tab, select the check box, and then click OK.

3. Select the sentence by holding down Ctrl and Shift simultaneously and then pressing the Right Arrow key until you have highlighted the entire sentence.

← Selecting a sentence

4. Point to the selected text, hold down the left mouse button, and drag the shadow insertion point to the right of the last period in the document's first paragraph (after *climber*). While still holding down the mouse button, hold down the Ctrl key (a small plus sign appears next to the mouse pointer), and then release first the mouse button and then the key. A copy of the selected sentence appears in the location designated by the shadow insertion point, as shown here:

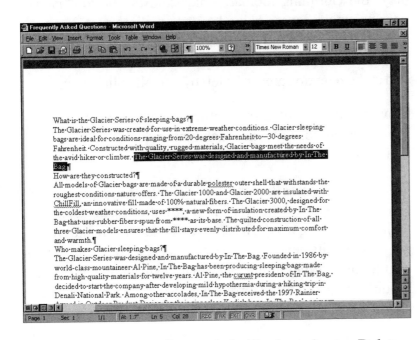

5. With the sentence you just copied still selected, press Delete.

Organizing Documents

You have seen how to move text around in a document using cut-and-paste and drag-and-drop editing, but when a document has headings as well as ordinary text, it's often simpler to use Word's Outlining feature to move things around. Most people are accustomed to thinking of outlining as the process that precedes the writing of lengthy documents. With Word, however, outlining is not a separate process but simply another way of looking at a document. If all you ever do is write

Extend-selection mode

You can use the extend-selection mode as another way to select text. Click an insertion point where you want the selection to start and then turn on extend-selection mode by pressing F8 or double-clicking the letters *EXT* in the status bar. Then click where you want the selection to end, and Word highlights all the text between the insertion point and the spot you clicked. To turn off extend-selection mode, simply press Esc or double-click the letters *EXT* in the status bar.

letters, memos, and other short documents, you may never use outlining. But if you write longer documents with headings, such as business plans, company reports, or term papers, outlining provides a powerful way of quickly organizing and reorganizing your information. Once you use Word's Outlining feature with a particular document, you can switch to outline view at any time to get an overview of your work.

In this section, we'll set up the outline for the FAQ and then use it to reorganize the document. Let's get started:

Turning on outlining

1. Choose Outline from the expanded View menu. Word displays the Outlining toolbar, which allows you to organize your document by assigning levels to the information on the screen. Because Word considers all the headings and paragraphs of the FAQ to be ordinary body text, each one is identified in the selection area to its left by a small hollow square.

2. Move the pointer over the Outlining toolbar, using Screen-Tips to get an idea of what each button does, and then press Ctrl+End to move to the end of the document.

The Promote button

3. On a new line, type *Glacier Sleeping Bags--Frequently Asked Questions*, and then click the Promote button on the Outlining toolbar. Word moves the heading to the left and makes it bigger to reflect its new status. Also notice the large minus icon next to the heading; it indicates that the heading has no subheadings or text. (AutoCorrect has also replaced the two hyphens with an em-dash—a dash the width of an *m*.)

Heading styles

4. Click the Formatting toolbar's More Buttons button and notice that Heading 1 appears in the Style box. (See page 75 for more information about styles.) Word can handle up to nine heading levels, called Heading 1 through Heading 9.

5. Click an insertion point in the *How do I order?* heading and then click the Promote button. Repeat this step for each of the remaining headings to change them to the Heading 1 style.

The Show Heading 1 button

6. Click the Show Heading 1 button. Word collapses the outline so that only the level 1 headings are visible, as shown here:

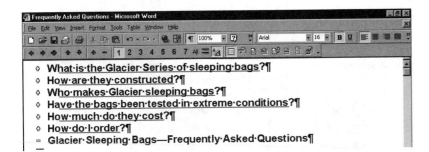

As we've already mentioned, a minus icon indicates that the heading doesn't have subordinate headings or text; a plus icon indicates that it does. In addition, Word puts a gray underline below headings whose subordinate information is hidden.

Now let's do a little reorganizing:

1. Click anywhere in the *Glacier Sleeping Bags—Frequently Asked Questions* heading and then click the Move Up button repeatedly until the heading is at the top of the document.

2. Click an insertion point in the *How are they constructed?* heading and then click the Move Down button once to move the heading below the *Who makes Glacier sleeping bags?* heading.

3. Click the Expand button to display the paragraph below the selected heading. As you can see on the next page, the paragraph has moved with its heading.

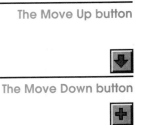

Outline symbols

The Move Up button

The Move Down button

The Expand button

Using the document map

Another way to view your Word documents is by using the document map. Click the Document Map button on the Standard toolbar to display the document map, which contains all of the headings of the document, in a separate pane on the left side of the screen. To move to a different heading, click the heading in the document map pane. That heading moves to the top of the pane on the right. To change the level of display in the document map, click a minus sign to collapse subheadings under a main heading. To redisplay subheadings, click a plus sign. For more specific levels of display, right-click a heading and choose an option from the shortcut menu. To resize the document map pane, move the pointer to the dividing line between the left and right panes, and when the pointer changes to a double-headed arrow, drag in the appropriate direction. To close the document map, either click the Document Map button or double-click the dividing line between the left and right panes.

Deleting headings

To delete a heading from an outline, select the heading and press Delete. If you want to also delete the heading's subordinate headings and text, collapse the outline before you make your selection. Otherwise, expand the outline before you select the heading so that you can see exactly which paragraphs will be affected when you press Delete.

The Collapse button

→ 4. Click the Collapse button to hide the text again.

What happens if you want to add information to the document while you are in outline view? Simple! Follow these steps:

1. Click an insertion point at the end of the *How are they constructed?* heading and press Enter. Word assumes you want to type another level 1 heading.

2. Type *Where are the bags made?* and press Enter.

The Demote To Body Text button

→ 3. Click the Demote To Body Text button on the Outlining toolbar and type the following, including the errors in bold:

   *All **materiuls** used in g-F3 bags are made in the USA. The bags are **assembulled** in our manufacturing plant in Anchorage, Alaska.*

Creating master documents and subdocuments

In outline view, you can create a master document that contains separate but related subdocuments. For example, if you want each question and answer of the FAQ to be contained in a separate subdocument, display the document in outline view, select a heading and its text, and click the Create Subdocument button on the Outlining toolbar. Repeat this procedure for all the other headings and their text to convert them to subdocuments. When you save the FAQ file, Word saves each subdocument as a separate file with the heading as the filename. In the FAQ master document, click the Collapse Subdocuments button to see only the headings, which have been converted to hyperlinks. Click the hyperlink for a heading to display its subdocument. This feature is particularly useful if you want to publish your documents for viewing over the Internet or an intranet (see page 84). For more information about master documents and subdocuments, see Word's Help feature.

Notice that all the headings except the first should really be level 2. Here's how to bump the headings down one level:

1. Click the Show Heading 1 button to display only the headings.

2. Select all the headings except the first and click the Demote button on the Outlining toolbar. Word both changes their formatting and moves the selected headings to the right so that their relationship to the level 1 heading is readily apparent. The minus icon to the left of the first heading changes to a plus icon because it now has subordinate headings and text.

The Demote button

3. Click the Show All Headings button to see these results:

The Show All Headings button

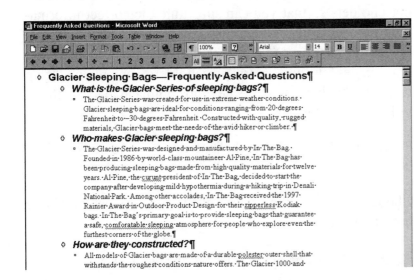

Well, after that brief introduction to Word's Outlining feature, let's switch to normal view so that you can move on with the rest of the chapter. By default, Word is in print layout view which displays your document as it will look on a printed page and shows headers and footers as well as other page elements. Normal view displays all of the text while simplifying the page layout to make typing and editing much easier. Here's how to make the switch:

Switching views

1. Click the Normal View button at the left end of the horizontal scroll bar. Having set up the document's outline, you can return to outline view at any time by simply clicking the Outline View button at the left end of the horizontal scroll bar.

The Normal View and Outline View buttons

2. Click the Save button to save your work.

Finding and Replacing

With Word, you can search a document for specific characters. You can also specify replacement characters. As you'll see if you follow along with the next example, finding a series of characters is easy.

Finding Text

Recall that while typing the Glacier sleeping bag FAQ, you left the characters **** as placeholders for information that needed to be added later. Suppose you now need to locate the placeholders so that you can substitute the correct information. In a document as short as the FAQ, you would have no difficulty locating ****. But if the current document were many pages long and several placeholders were involved, you would probably want to use the Find command to locate them. Follow these steps:

The Find command →

1. Press Ctrl+Home to move the insertion point to the top of the document.

2. Choose Find from the Edit menu. Word displays the dialog box shown here:

Editing during a search or replace

To edit a document without closing the Find And Replace dialog box, click the document window to activate it, make your changes, and then click anywhere in the Find And Replace dialog box to continue the search or replace. You can also click the Cancel button to close the Find And Replace dialog box and instead use the Next Find/GoTo and Previous Find/GoTo buttons at the bottom of the vertical scroll bar to complete your search without the dialog box in your way.

3. Enter **** in the Find What edit box and click Find Next. Word searches the document, stopping when it locates the first occurrence of ****.

4. Click Cancel to close the dialog box and then type *CozyTec* to replace the highlighted placeholder.

5. Click the Next Find/GoTo button at the bottom of the vertical scroll bar to repeat the Find command using the same Find What text as the previous search. Word locates the second ****. (You can click the Previous Find/GoTo button to go back to the previous instance of the Find What text.)

The Next Find/GoTo and Previous Find/GoTo buttons

6. Replace the selection with *recycled tires*.

Most of your searches will be as simple as this one was, but you can also refine your searches by first clicking the More button in the Find And Replace dialog box to display additional options. You can then use these options or enter special characters (see the tip on page 51). For example, suppose you regularly confuse the two words *further* and *farther*. You can check your use of these words in the FAQ, as follows:

1. Press Ctrl+Home to move to the top of the document. Then click the Select Browse Object button at the bottom of the vertical scroll bar to display this palette of options:

The Select Browse Object button

> **· How·are·they·constructed?¶**
> All·models·of·Glacier·bags·are·made·of·a·durable·polester·outer·shell·that·withstands·the·
> roughest·conditions·nature·offers.·The·Glacier·1000·and·Glacier·2000·are·insulated·with·
> ChillFill,·an·innovative·fill·made·of·100%·natural·fibers.·The·Glacier·3000,·designed·for·
> the·coldest·weather·conditions,·uses·CozyTec,·a·new·form·of·insulation·created·by·In·The·
> Bag·that·uses·rubber·fibers·spun·from·recycled·tires·as·its·base.·The·quilted·construction·

These buttons allow you to browse through your document by heading, graphic, table and so on.

2. Click the Find button to display the Find And Replace dialog box again.

The Find button

3. Next click the More button to expand the Find And Replace dialog box, as shown on the next page.

Finding and replacing formats

To search for text with an assigned format, choose Find from the Edit menu, click the More button to expand the Find And Replace dialog box, click the Format button, and then click Font (for character formats) or Paragraph. In the Find Font or Find Paragraph dialog box, specify the format you seek, click OK to return to the Find And Replace dialog box, and click Find Next. Word highlights the next text entry with the assigned format. You can use the Replace command to change a particular format. For example, to change all bold text to bold italic, choose Replace from the Edit menu, click Format and then Font, click Bold in the Font Style list, and click OK. Then click the Replace With edit box, click Format and then Font. In the Font Style list, click Bold Italic and click OK. Back in the Find And Replace dialog box, click Find Next and Replace, if you want to confirm each change, or click Replace All.

```
Find and Replace                                            ? X
  Find  │ Replace │ Go To │
  Find what: │****                                      │▼│

                                    ┌─────────┐ ┌──────────┐ ┌────────┐
                                    │ Less ±  │ │ Find Next│ │ Cancel │
                                    └─────────┘ └──────────┘ └────────┘
  Search Options
    Search:      │All        ▼│
      ☐ Match case
      ☐ Find whole words only
      ☐ Use wildcards
      ☐ Sounds like
      ☐ Find all word forms
  Find
          ┌──────────┐ ┌──────────┐ ┌───────────────┐
          │ Format ▼ │ │ Special ▼│ │ No Formatting │
          └──────────┘ └──────────┘ └───────────────┘
```

Wildcards

4. Enter *f?rthe* in the Find What edit box. The ? is a *wildcard* character that stands for any single character.

5. Check that All is selected as the Search option. Then click Use Wildcards to tell Word to look for a string of characters that matches the Find What text, and click Find Next to start the search. Word stops at the word *furthest* in the second paragraph. (You may need to move the dialog box by dragging its title bar so that you can see the text.)

6. This use of *furthest* is incorrect, so click Cancel to close the dialog box and change the *u* to *a*.

7. Click the Next Find/GoTo button to repeat the search. Word stops at the word *further*, which is correct.

8. Click the Next Find/GoTo button again to ensure that the document contains no other instances of the Find What text, and click No when Word asks whether you want to continue the search.

Replacing Text

The Go To tab

You can use the Go To tab of the Find And Replace dialog box to jump to a specific element in your document. For example, you can move to a specific page, graphic or heading.

Often, you will search a document for a series of characters with the intention of replacing them. When you need to make the same replacement more than a couple of times, using the Replace command automates the process. As an example, let's find all the occurrences of *Glacier bags* and change them to *Glacier sleeping bags*:

1. Press Ctrl+Home to move to the beginning of the document, click the Select Browse Object button, click Find, and click the Replace tab. (You can also use the Replace command on the Edit menu.) Word displays the dialog box shown here:

Notice that the text and settings from the Find tab have been carried over to the Replace tab.

2. Replace the Find What text by typing *Glacier bags*.

3. In the Replace With edit box, type *Glacier sleeping bags*. Click the Less button to decrease the size of the dialog box, and click Find Next. Word highlights the first occurrence of the Find What text.

4. Click Replace. Word continues the search and highlights the second occurrence.

5. Click Replace All to replace any remaining occurrences, and then click OK when Word tells you that four replacements have been made.

6. Click Close to close the Find And Replace dialog box.

As with the Find command, you can use the Match Case, Find Whole Words Only, Use Wildcards, Sounds Like, and Find All Word Forms options to refine the replace procedure. (See the adjacent tip for more information.)

Refining your searches

By using the options available in the Find And Replace dialog box, you can complete more complicated searches in your Word documents. Use the options in the Search drop-down list to search forward (Down) or backward (Up) from the insertion point, or to search the entire document (All). Click the Match Case check box to find only those occurrences of the Find What text with the exact capitalization specified. For example, find the initials *USA* and not the characters *usa* in *usability*. Click the Find Whole Words Only check box to find only whole-word occurrences of the Find What text. For example, find the word *men* and not the characters *men* in *fundamental*. Find special characters, such as tabs and paragraph marks, by selecting them from the Special drop-down list. For example, find the paragraphs that begin with *Remember* by selecting Paragraph Mark from the list and then typing *Remember* after ^p as the Find What text. Click the Sounds Like check box to find occurrences of the Find What text that sound the same but are spelled differently. Finally, click the Find All Word Forms check box to find occurrences of a particular word in any form. For example, if the Find What text is the word *hide*, Word will also find *hid* and *hidden*. (You may need to install this feature before you can use it.)

Checking Spelling and Grammar

Nothing detracts from a document like a typo. In the past, readers might have overlooked the occasional misspelling. These days, running a word processor's spelling checker is so easy that readers tend to be less forgiving. For example, résumés and job-application letters with typos often go in the recycling bin. The moral: You should get in the habit of spell-checking all your documents, especially before distributing printed copies.

As we created the FAQ in this chapter, we deliberately included a few errors. By default, Word checks the spelling of each word you type against its built-in dictionary and flags with a red, wavy underline any word it does not find. It also checks for grammatical errors, flagging them with a green, wavy underline. These features, called *automatic spell checking* and *automatic grammar checking*, can be turned on or off on the Spelling & Grammar tab of the Options dialog box. (You might want to check out the other spelling and grammar options on this tab.)

Usually you will want to correct any errors Word identifies as you go along. Let's fix one of the misspelled words now:

1. Point to the word *curunt* in the FAQ's second body-text paragraph and right-click it to display this shortcut menu:

Automatic spell and grammar checking

Using the Spelling And Grammar Status icon

If you want to move from one spelling or grammar error to the next without displaying the Spelling And Grammar dialog box, you can do so by using the Spelling And Grammar Status icon in the status bar. To highlight the first potential error and display its shortcut menu of options, double-click the Spelling And Grammar Status icon (the open book with the red X). To move to the next potential error, double-click that icon again. When Word finds no other errors in the document, the red X in the icon becomes a check mark, indicating the spelling and grammar check is complete.

Word displays any words in its dictionary that come close to the offending text. It also gives you the options of ignoring the misspelling, adding the word to a supplemental dictionary, creating an AutoCorrect entry for the word, changing the language used, or displaying the Spelling And Grammar dialog box, which offers more options.

2. Click *current* to change the word to its correct spelling.

   If you prefer to check the spelling of a document all at once, you can use Word's spell-checking capabilities in another way:

1. Press Ctrl+Home to move to the top of the FAQ, and click the Spelling And Grammar button on the Standard toolbar. Word automatically begins checking each word of the document, starting with the word containing the insertion point, against its built-in dictionary. When it finds a word that is not in its dictionary, Word highlights the word and displays this Spelling And Grammar dialog box:

The Spelling And Grammar button

2. As you can see, Word stopped at the word *zipperless*. Although this term is not in Word's dictionary, it is correct, so click Ignore All. (The red, wavy underline disappears from every occurrence of the word.)

3. Next Word questions *comforatable*—a genuine misspelling. Click Change to accept the suggestion that Word offers, *comfortable*.

4. Word comes to *polester* and suggests *polestar*. Click *polyester* in the Suggestions list and then click Change.

5. Next Word stops on *ChillFill*. You have spelled this name correctly and use it often. To prevent Word from flagging it as a misspelling every time, add it to Word's supplemental dictionary, Custom.dic, by clicking the Add button. (You cannot add words to the main dictionary.) Repeat this procedure to add *CozyTec* to the supplemental dictionary.

6. As Word continues the spell check, change *materiuls* to *materials* and *assembulled* to *assembled*. When Word flags the company e-mail address, click Add to add the address to the supplemental dictionary.

7. When Word reaches the end of the document, it closes the Spelling And Grammar dialog box and displays a message that the spelling and grammar check is complete. Click OK to return to your document.

8. Save and then close the document. (You will use it again in Chapter 3.) Then close Word.

As you create documents and spell-check them, you will start to see that the words you use fall into several categories:

• Common words that are included in Word's main dictionary.

• Uncommon words that you use rarely. You will want to tell Word to ignore these when spell-checking a document. Word

Smart checking

If your document contains duplicate words, such as *the the*, Word displays them in the Spelling And Grammar dialog box during a spelling and grammar check. Clicking Delete removes the duplicate word. To speed up the checking process, Word's suggestions generally have the same case as a misspelled word. For example, if the misspelling occurs at the beginning of a sentence and starts with a capital letter, Word's suggestions also start with capital letters.

Checking grammar

As we've said, when automatic grammar checking is turned on, Word works behind the scenes, checking your grammar as you type and underlining suspicious phrases with green, wavy underlines. Right-clicking underlined phrases displays a shortcut menu with suggested changes. You can also click Ignore to leave the phrase as is or click Grammar to display the Grammar dialog box for more options. The usefulness of the grammar checker depends on the complexity of your writing. Only you can decide whether its suggestions are valid and helpful enough to warrant leaving it turned on. If you want to spell-check your documents without using Word's Grammar checker, choose Options from the Tools menu, display the Spelling And Grammar tab, and then deselect the Check Grammar As You Type and Check Grammar With Spelling check boxes.

will then attach those words to the document in which they are used as a sort of document-specific dictionary and will not flag them as misspellings if you spell-check the document in the future.

- Uncommon words that you use often in different kinds of documents. You will want to add these words to Custom.dic so that they are not flagged as misspellings.

- Uncommon words that you use with a specific type of document. Instead of adding these words to Custom.dic, you might want to create a custom dictionary for use only with that type of document. To create a custom dictionary, choose Options from the Tools menu, click the Spelling & Grammar tab, click the Dictionaries button, and then click the New button in the Custom Dictionaries dialog box. Type a name for the dictionary, click Save, and then click OK. Before you can use the custom dictionary, you must open it by selecting it from the drop-down list in the Options dialog box and clicking OK. (You can also create and open custom dictionaries on the Spelling & Grammar tab that appears when you click Options in the Spelling And Grammar dialog box.) Then when you check a document's spelling, you can click the Add button in the Spelling And Grammar dialog box to add words to the custom dictionary. (Before starting a spelling check, it is a good idea to click the Options button and check which custom dictionary is in effect.)

Creating custom dictionaries

You can't rely on Word's spelling and grammar checker to identify every error in your documents. Errors of syntax or improper word usage can easily slip by in a spelling and grammar check. You should always read through your documents to look for any errors that Word might miss.

The Thesaurus

You can use the Word Thesaurus to look up synonyms for a selected word by choosing Language and then Thesaurus from the Tools menu. (You may need to install the Thesaurus first.) The Thesaurus dialog box suggests alternative words for the selected word. Select the new word in the Replace With Synonym list and click the Replace button. You can also select an alternative word and click Look Up to display a list of alternatives for the alternative.

Eye-Catching Documents

You create a memo and a fax as you explore Word's built-in templates and wizards. Then you combine two documents and try out more complex formats, such as multiple columns, lists, and styles. Finally, you learn to print documents on paper and publish them on the Web.

Whether your document is a flyer like our example or a business advertisement or club newsletter, adding fancy formatting is an effective way to get your work noticed.

Documents created and concepts covered:

Use a template to create an impressive memo

Set off paragraphs with first line indents and space above and below

Dress up headings with borders

Turn formatting combinations into styles

Use multi-column formats to vary document design

Use autoformatting to quickly create numbered and bulleted lists

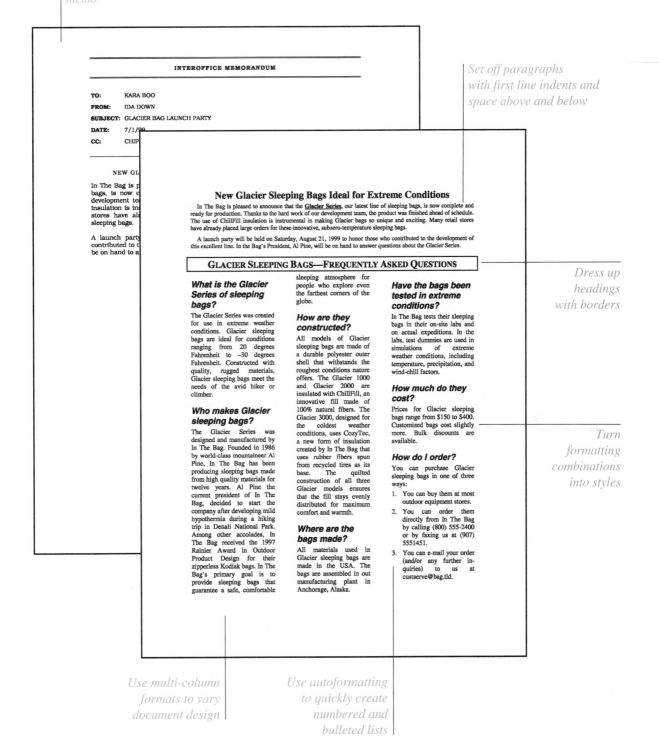

INTEROFFICE MEMORANDUM

TO: KARA BOO
FROM: IDA DOWN
SUBJECT: GLACIER BAG LAUNCH PARTY
DATE: 7/1/99
CC: CHIP

NEW GL

In The Bag is p
bags, is now c
development te
insulation is ins
stores have al
sleeping bags.

A launch party
contributed to t
be on hand to a

New Glacier Sleeping Bags Ideal for Extreme Conditions

In The Bag is pleased to announce that the **Glacier Series**, our latest line of sleeping bags, is now complete and ready for production. Thanks to the hard work of our development team, the product was finished ahead of schedule. The use of ChillFill insulation is instrumental in making Glacier bags so unique and exciting. Many retail stores have already placed large orders for these innovative, subzero-temperature sleeping bags.

A launch party will be held on Saturday, August 21, 1999 to honor those who contributed to the development of this excellent line. In The Bag's President, Al Pine, will be on hand to answer questions about the Glacier Series.

GLACIER SLEEPING BAGS—FREQUENTLY ASKED QUESTIONS

What is the Glacier Series of sleeping bags?

The Glacier Series was created for use in extreme weather conditions. Glacier sleeping bags are ideal for conditions ranging from 20 degrees Fahrenheit to –30 degrees Fahrenheit. Constructed with quality, rugged materials, Glacier sleeping bags meet the needs of the avid hiker or climber.

Who makes Glacier sleeping bags?

The Glacier Series was designed and manufactured by In The Bag. Founded in 1986 by world-class mountaineer Al Pine, In The Bag has been producing sleeping bags made from high quality materials for twelve years. Al Pine the current president of In The Bag, decided to start the company after developing mild hypothermia during a hiking trip in Denali National Park. Among other accolades, In The Bag received the 1997 Rainier Award in Outdoor Product Design for their zipperless Kodiak bags. In The Bag's primary goal is to provide sleeping bags that guarantee a safe, comfortable

sleeping atmosphere for people who explore even the farthest corners of the globe.

How are they constructed?

All models of Glacier sleeping bags are made of a durable polyester outer shell that withstands the roughest conditions nature offers. The Glacier 1000 and Glacier 2000 are insulated with ChillFill, an innovative fill made of 100% natural fibers. The Glacier 3000, designed for the coldest weather conditions, uses CozyTec, a new form of insulation created by In The Bag that uses rubber fibers spun from recycled tires as its base. The quilted construction of all three Glacier models ensures that the fill stays evenly distributed for maximum comfort and warmth.

Where are the bags made?

All materials used in Glacier sleeping bags are made in the USA. The bags are assembled in out manufacturing plant in Anchorage, Alaska.

Have the bags been tested in extreme conditions?

In The Bag tests their sleeping bags in their on-site labs and on actual expeditions. In the labs, test dummies are used in simulations of extreme weather conditions, including temperature, precipitation, and wind-chill factors.

How much do they cost?

Prices for Glacier sleeping bags range from $150 to $400. Customized bags cost slightly more. Bulk discounts are available.

How do I order?

You can purchase Glacier sleeping bags in one of three ways:

1. You can buy them at most outdoor equipment stores.
2. You can order them directly from In The Bag by calling (800) 555-2400 or by faxing us at (907) 5551451.
3. You can e-mail your order (and/or any further inquiries) to us at custserve@bag.tld.

This chapter focuses on ways to produce documents with eye-appeal. First you use Word's ready-made templates and wizards to create professional-looking documents without having to fuss with formatting. Then you explore the Word capabilities that can give all your documents that professional touch. Finally, we show you how to publish your documents either on paper or on the Web.

Using Word's Templates

A *template* is a pattern that includes the information, formatting, and other elements used in a particular type of document. Unless you specify otherwise, all new Word documents are based on the Blank Document template. But Word comes with several other templates that you can use as is or modify; or you can create your own templates (see the tip on page 60).

The default template →

As part of the Word installation procedure, several templates were copied to the Templates subfolder of the Program Files\Microsoft Office folder on your hard drive. To preview the templates, follow these steps:

The Print Layout View button →

1. Start Word. If necessary, switch to print layout view by clicking the Print Layout View button at the bottom of the window.

2. Check that both the rulers and nonprinting characters are displayed. (Choose Ruler from the View menu and click the Show/Hide ¶ button.)

3. Choose New from the File menu to display this dialog box:

Install on demand

If a preview is not available for a particular template or wizard in the New dialog box, you can easily install it. Select the template or wizard and then click OK. Word may prompt you to insert the installation CD-ROM and then starts the installation process. When this process is complete, Word opens a document based on the template or starts the wizard. This install-on-demand capability allows you to install items as you need them rather than having to store items on your hard drive that you may never need to use.

Word organizes its templates in categories on different tabs. The default selection (which is available even when no other templates have been installed) is Blank Document on the General tab.

4. On the Letters & Faxes tab, click Contemporary Letter to highlight it. If this template is installed, the Preview box on the right side of the dialog box shows a preview of it. If it is not installed, you can install it by clicking OK.

◄—————————————————

Previewing templates

5. Click more templates on the Letters & Faxes tab and then switch to some of the other tabs. As you can tell from their names and previews, the templates provide the basis for several common business documents.

6. When you are ready, select Elegant Memo on the Memos tab, and either press Enter or click OK. Word displays this memo form on your screen:

Date fields

Word automatically enters the date stored by your system's clock/calendar when you open a document based on the memo template. Why? Because the document contains a special code called a *field*. Fields can contain a variety of information; this particular field instructs Word to get the current date and display it in the field's location. If you do nothing to this field, Word will insert the current date each time you open the document. If you want to "freeze" the current date, click the field to select it and press Ctrl+Shift+F9. The field is converted to normal text that will not be updated and that can be edited. To insert a date field in a document, choose Date And Time from the Insert menu, and in the Date And Time dialog box, select a date format, click the Update Automatically check box to select it, and click OK.

As you can see, all the common elements of a memo have placeholders within square brackets, and Word has entered the current date (using the date stored in your computer—see the adjacent tip). Let's fill in the memo now.

1. In the To section, click the placeholder text to select it and its square brackets, and type *Kara Boo*. Because of the formatting applied to the placeholder, the name appears in capital letters even though you typed it with initial capitals only.

2. In the From section, type *Ida Down*, and in the Subject section, type *Glacier Bag Launch Party*.

3. Finally, in the CC: section, type *Chip Monk*.

4. Now select the title *How to Use This Memo Template* and replace it with *New Glacier Sleeping Bags Ideal for Extreme Conditions*.

   Take a moment to admire your work. Without adding any formatting of your own, you've created a professional-looking header for a memo, as shown here:

Creating custom templates

You can save any document as a template for future use. First choose Save As from the File menu, click the arrow to the right of the Save As Type box, and select Document Template. Word moves to the C:\Windows\Application Data\Microsoft\Templates folder. Assign a name to the template in the File Name edit box and click Save. To use the new template, choose New from the File menu and select the template the same way you would select any of Word's templates.

5. Choose Save As from the File menu and save the document with the name *Glacier Memo*.

Below the memo title, you need to enter the text of the memo. This information is essentially the same as that contained in the letter you wrote in Chapter 1. The beauty of a word processor like Word is that instead of retyping the information, you can borrow it from the letter and edit it to suit the purpose of the memo. Here's how:

1. Select the text of the main paragraph (but not the paragraph mark) and press the Delete key.

2. To open the letter from Chapter 1 in its own window, click the Open button on the toolbar, and in the Open dialog box, double-click Launch Party Letter.

3. Select the two main paragraphs of the letter, including the paragraph mark between them, and click the Copy button.

4. Next click the Glacier Memo button on the Windows taskbar to switch to that document's window and then press Ctrl+End to make sure the insertion point is in the blank paragraph at the end of the memo.

5. Click the Paste button to insert the copied text.

6. Edit the text of the memo so that it looks like the one shown below. (We've magnified the memo so that the text is more readable.)

Don't worry for now that the formatting of the second paragraph looks different from that of the first. You'll fix it on page 77.

7. Save the document and then close it.

8. Close Launch Party Letter, clicking No if Word asks whether you want to save any changes.

What's the big deal about paragraph marks?

You may have noticed in the examples in this chapter that we often tell you when to select or delete paragraph marks. When using templates, you are dealing with text that has been preformatted, and often the formatting is stored with the paragraph mark. If the paragraph mark is deleted, you risk losing all of the preset formatting, in which case you'll have to reformat the text from scratch.

Using Word's Wizards

When you create a new document based on a wizard, the wizard makes multiple—and often complex—decisions based on your answers to its questions. Let's use the Fax Wizard to create a fax to announce In The Bag's new line of Glacier sleeping bags:

Creating a fax

1. Choose New from the File menu, click the Letters & Faxes tab, and double-click Fax Wizard to display the wizard's first dialog box. (If the Fax Wizard is not installed, you may be prompted to insert your installation CD-ROM; see the tip on page 58.)

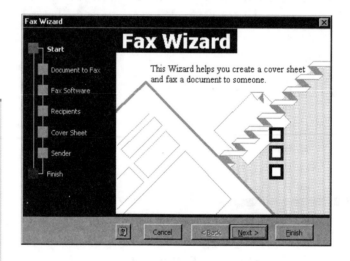

Wizards

Wizards are tools that are incorporated into Word to help you accomplish specific tasks. They all work in the same basic way, regardless of the task. Each consists of a series of dialog boxes asking you to provide information or to select from various options. You move from box to box by clicking the Next button, and you can move back to an earlier box by clicking the Back button. Clicking Cancel aborts the entire procedure. Clicking Finish tells the wizard to complete the task with the current settings. Some wizards, like the Fax Wizard, include a "road map" with colored boxes representing the wizard's steps. You can see exactly where you are in the process by glancing at the boxes, and you can jump to a particular step by clicking its box.

2. Click Next to display the second dialog box:

3. Confirm that the Just A Cover Sheet With A Note option is selected, and then click Next to display the wizard's third dialog box, shown here:

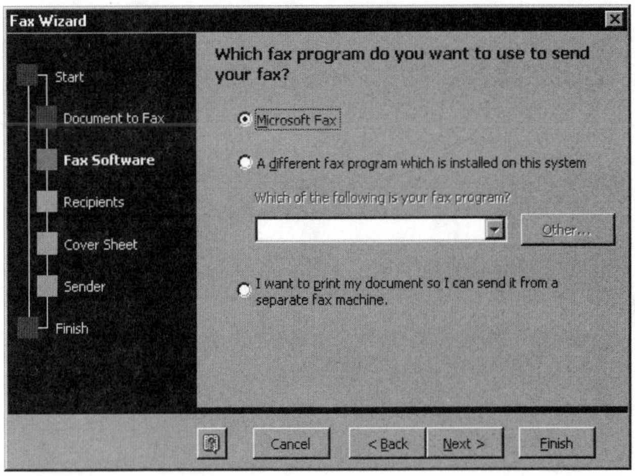

4. Click the third option so that you can print the document and send it from a separate fax machine. Then click Next to display this dialog box:

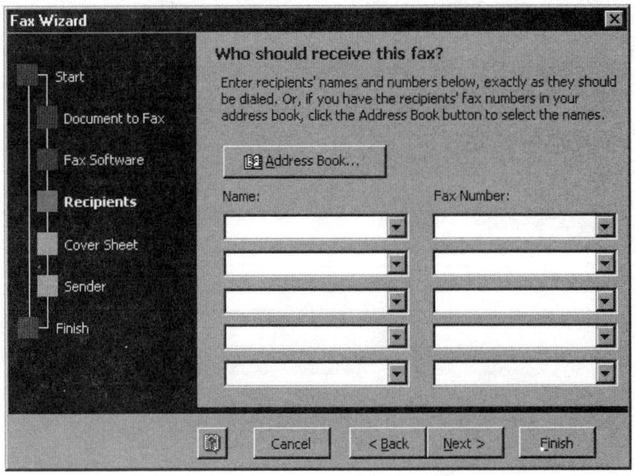

Here you can select names and numbers from an electronic address book (see the tip on the next page), or you can type the names and numbers manually. (If the Fax Wizard has been used before, the names of recent fax recipients may appear in the drop-down lists.)

More Fax Wizard options

You can send a fax to several people at once by filling in their names and numbers in the fourth dialog box (or using an electronic address book). After you've completed all of the wizard's dialog boxes, Word displays the fax along with the Mail Merge toolbar. The names and numbers you included are now merge fields. To view the fields, click the View Merged Data button found on the Mail Merge toolbar and then cycle through the faxes by clicking the Next Record or Previous Record button. To print the faxes, click the Merge To Printer button on the Mail Merge toolbar. To send faxes directly from your computer, you must have access to a modem on your computer or on your network. Select your fax program in the third Fax Wizard dialog box. When Word displays the fax, you can complete it and click the Send Fax Now button.

5. With the insertion point located in the top Name box, type *Fern Leaf*, press Tab, type *(907) 555-1201*, and click Next to display the dialog box shown here:

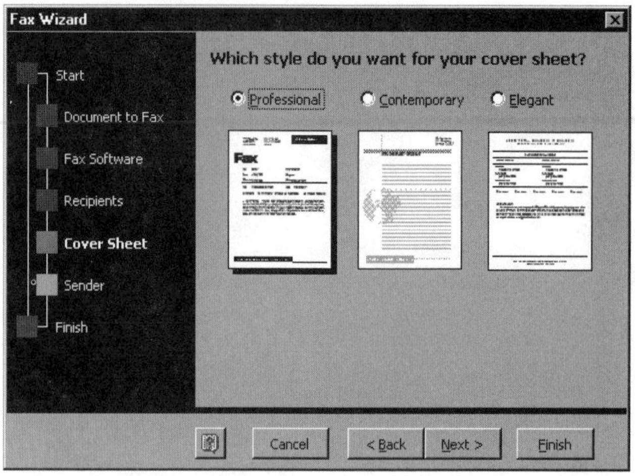

6. With the Professional option selected, click Next to display this dialog box:

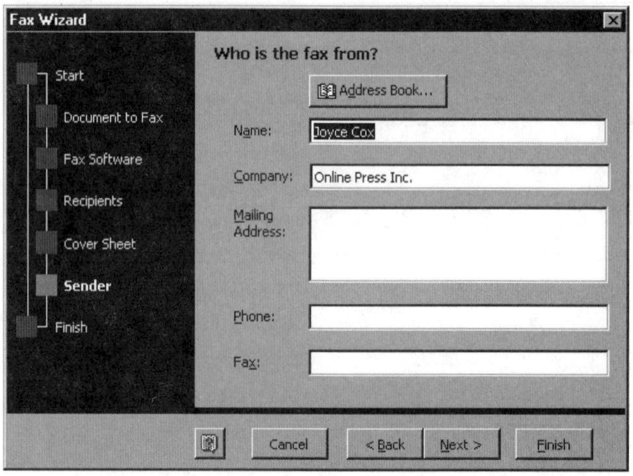

Using an electronic address book

When creating a fax using the Fax Wizard, you may want to access addresses entered in an electronic address book, such as the Microsoft Outlook address book. To access it from the Fax Wizard, click the Address Book button in the fourth wizard dialog box and if necessary choose a profile. Word opens the address book and lets you select the name(s) you want.

7. In the Name box, type *Al Pine*. Then enter this information, pressing Tab to move from box to box:

Company:	*In The Bag*
Mailing Address:	*1200 Yukon Ave.* (Press Enter)
	Anchorage, AK 99502
Phone:	*(907) 555-1450*
Fax:	*(907) 555-1451*

8. Click Finish to display these results (we've changed the screen magnification so that you can see the entire fax):

Complete the fax header by following these steps:

1. Replace the Phone placeholder with *(907) 555-1200* and the Pages placeholder with *1*.

2. Next type *Glacier Series* as the subject, and delete the CC placeholder.

3. Double-click the box to the left of Please Reply. Word responds by putting a check mark in the box, like this:

Now let's insert the text of the fax:

1. Delete the entire Comments line, but not the paragraph mark.

What produces the check mark?

The check boxes at the bottom of the fax cover-sheet header are actually fields with a *macro*, or small program, attached to them. Double-clicking a check box runs the macro, which instructs Word to insert a check mark in the box. The topic of macros is beyond the scope of this book, but you can get more information by reading the discussions of macros in Word's Help feature.

2. Open Glacier Memo (the document you created in the last section), select the two main paragraphs, click the Copy button, and close the memo.

3. With the insertion point at the end of the fax document, click the Paste button.

4. Save the fax with the name *7-01-99 Fax* (or the date of your fax) and then close it.

More Formatting Techniques

As you saw in the previous chapter, a well-designed document uses formatting to provide visual cues about its structure. In this section, you'll explore some more formatting techniques as you combine the FAQ from Chapter 2 and the memo from this chapter to make a flyer. Follow these steps:

1. With a blank window on your screen, click the Open button on the Standard toolbar and double-click Frequently Asked Questions in the My Documents folder.

2. To safeguard the original FAQ file, choose Save As from the File menu and save the current version as *Flyer*.

3. If necessary, switch to print layout view.

4. Press Ctrl+Home to be sure that the insertion point is at the top of the document, and choose File from the expanded Insert menu to display this Insert File dialog box:

Painting formats

If you want to format a block of text with settings that you have already applied to another block of text, you can copy all the formatting in a simple three-step procedure. Select the text whose settings you want to copy, click the Format Painter button on the Standard toolbar, and then select the text you want to format. Word duplicates the formatting for the new selection. To format more than one block of text, double-click the Format Painter button, select each block in turn, and then click the button to turn it off.

5. Select Glacier Memo from the list of documents and click Insert to merge its file into Flyer.

6. Press Ctrl+Home to move to the top of the combined document, and select and delete the entire memo header. Then delete the blank paragraph at the end of the memo, leaving only the two main paragraphs and the paragraph mark between them.

7. Click the Save button on the toolbar to save the combined document, which looks like this:

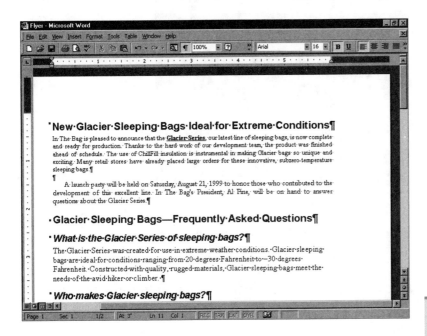

From now on, we won't tell you when to save the flyer, but you should do so at regular intervals to safeguard your work.

Making Titles Stand Out

As you know, you apply character formatting when you want to change the appearance of individual characters. Here you'll focus on the titles of the two "articles" in the new flyer. Let's get started:

1. Move to the top of the document, select the title of the memo, click the Center button on the Formatting toolbar to center the title, and change the font to Times New Roman.

Rebreaking titles and headings

As you create titles and headings for your Word documents, you may find that some of them would be more aesthetically pleasing if they broke to multiple lines or broke in a different spot. To rebreak a title or heading (or any other line of text), simply click an insertion point in the place where you want the break to occur and press Shift+Enter. Word then inserts a line break, which it designates on the screen with a broken-arrow symbol.

2. Now select the title of the FAQ, including its paragraph mark. Center the title and change the font to Times New Roman.

3. With the title still selected, choose Font from the Format menu to display this dialog box:

As you can see, the dialog box reflects the character formatting of the selected title. It also provides several options not available on the Formatting toolbar.

4. Click Small Caps in the Effects section to format the title in small capital letters with large initial capital letters, and then click OK.

If you want, you can experiment with some of the other options in the Font dialog box before moving on.

Adding Borders and Shading

To emphasize particular paragraphs, you can draw lines above and below or to the left and right of them, or you can surround the paragraphs with different styles of borders. Put a border around the FAQ title now by following the steps on the facing page.

1. With the title still selected, choose Borders And Shading from the Format menu to display the dialog box shown here:

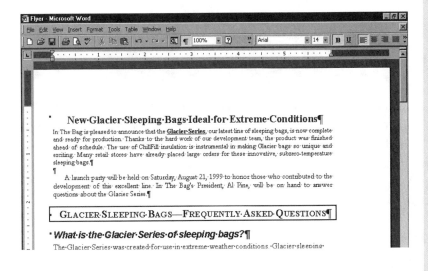

2. Click the arrow to the right of the Width box and select the 1½ pt single-line option.

Changing line styles

3. Click the Box setting. Word displays a preview on the right side of the dialog box.

4. Next click the Shading tab. In the Fill section, click a light color. (We left the box white for legibility.) Then click OK.

5. Click away from the title to remove the highlighting and see these results:

AutoFormat As You Type

By default, Word automatically formats certain elements of your documents, such as numbered lists. If you want to turn this feature off, choose AutoCorrect from the Tools menu and click the AutoFormat As You Type tab to view the settings available with this option. In the Apply As You Type section, deselect any of the features you want to turn off. In the Replace As You Type section, you can specify whether Word should turn straight quotes (" ") to smart quotes (" "), use superscript with ordinals (1st), use fraction characters (½), change placeholder symbol characters and formatting, and create hyperlinks for Internet and network paths. In the Automatically As You Type section, you can control the treatment of lists and styles.

6. If you want, experiment with the other possible border and shading options.

Setting Up Multiple Columns

Newsletters and flyers often feature multi-column layouts like those of magazines and newspapers. These layouts give you more flexibility when it comes to the placement of elements on the page, and they are often more visually interesting than single-column layouts. With Word, setting up multiple columns for an entire document couldn't be easier. You simply click the Columns button on the Standard toolbar and select the number of columns you want. And as you'll see if you follow these steps, when you want only part of a document to have a multi-column layout, you select that part of the document before clicking the Columns button:

1. Select the text beginning with *What is the Glacier Series of sleeping bags?* to the period in the very last sentence of the *How do I order?* paragraph. (Don't select the paragraph mark.)

The Columns button

2. Click the Columns button on the Standard toolbar. (You'll probably have to click the More Buttons button to see the button palette.) Word drops down this grid of columns:

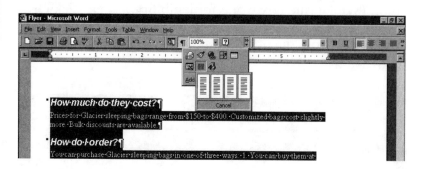

3. Point to the first column, move the mouse pointer over to the third column, and click. Word reformats the text so that it snakes across both the first and second page in three columns. Word puts a section break at the beginning of the selected text and another at the end. (See the adjacent tip for information about document sections.)

4. Press Home to move to the beginning of the selection. The document now looks like this:

Document sections

When applying different formatting—such as changing the number of columns or setting different margins—to only part of a document, Word designates the beginning and end of that part with section breaks that show up in some views as double dotted lines. You can insert section breaks manually by choosing Break from the Insert menu, selecting one of the options in the Section Break Types section, and then clicking OK. You can have the new section start at the top of the next new page, the next even page, or the next odd page; or you can have the new section continue immediately after the old section.

Creating Lists

The last paragraph of the FAQ contains three numbered items that would stand out better if they were set up as a list. Word has two built-in list formats: one for numbered lists and one for bulleted lists. Here's how to implement the numbered list format (the bulleted list format works the same way—see the tip on the next page for more information):

1. Use the scroll bar to move to the last paragraph on the second page, click an insertion point to the left of the number 1, and press Enter.

2. Click an insertion point to the left of the number 2 and press Enter. Word recognizes that consecutive paragraphs starting with numbers comprise a numbered list and responds by adding another 2 and a period in front of the new paragraph, giving both numbered paragraphs a hanging-indent format. This capability is called *AutoFormat As You Type* (see the tip on page 69).

3. Delete the extra 2, the period, and the space in the second numbered paragraph.

4. Repeat steps 2 and 3 for the number 3.

More column options

When you click the Columns button on the Standard toolbar and move the pointer across the grid in order to highlight the number of columns you want, you can select only up to four columns. However, if you hold down the left mouse button and then drag to make your selection, you can select up to six columns. To format columns precisely, choose Columns from the Format menu to display the Columns dialog box. Here you can define the number of columns, the format, the width, the spacing, and whether you want to show a dividing line between the columns. As you make your selections, Word displays a preview of the column formatting in the Preview box.

5. The numbered list columns are pretty skinny. To adjust them, select the three paragraphs, choose Bullets And Numbering from the Format menu, and click the Customize button to display these options:

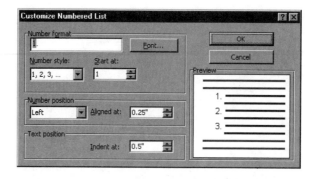

Bulleted lists

To create a bulleted list, select the paragraphs you want listed this way and click the Bullets button on the Formatting toolbar. You can also type an asterisk (*) and a space at the beginning of a new paragraph, and Word will convert the paragraph to a bulleted list as soon as you press Enter. (See the tip on page 69 for more information about this AutoFormat As You Type feature.) By default, Word precedes each paragraph with a large, round dot. To change this symbol, first select the bulleted paragraphs, then choose Bullets And Numbering from the Format menu, and select one of six other standard symbols. You can modify the format of bulleted and numbered lists by clicking the Customize button on their respective tabs, making your changes, and clicking OK. You can also click the Picture button to insert graphical bullets appropriate for Web page use.

6. Change the setting in the Aligned At box to 0, change the setting in the Indent At box to 0.25", and click OK. Then press End to see these results:

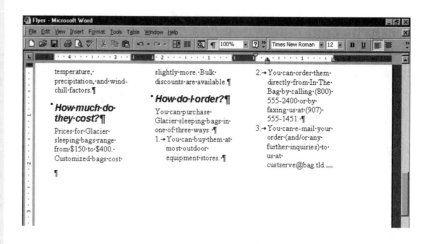

To create a numbered list from scratch, type 1, a period, a space, and the first numbered item, and press Enter. Word formats the next paragraph as the next item of the numbered list. To return to regular formatting, click the Numbering button on the Formatting toolbar. To convert existing text paragraphs to a numbered list, select the paragraphs and click the Numbering button.

Adding Headers and Footers

The flyer is currently two pages long. For documents that are longer than one page, you'll usually want to add a header or footer, so we'll show you how to do that next.

Headers are printed in the top margin of the page, and footers are printed in the bottom margin. With Word, you have many header and footer options. For example, you can create identical headers and footers for every page, a different header and footer for the first page, different headers and footers for left (even) pages and right (odd) pages, or different headers and footers for each section of a document.

Follow these steps to add a header to all the pages of the flyer except the first:

1. Press Ctrl+End to move to the end of the document, and press Ctrl+Enter to insert a page break, thereby creating a new page. (You can also choose Break from the Insert menu and accept the default Page Break option by clicking OK.) Your document now has three pages.

2. Press Ctrl+Home to move to the top of the flyer.

3. Choose Header And Footer from the View menu. Word dims the text of the document, outlines the space in which the header will appear with a dotted box, and displays the Header And Footer floating toolbar, as shown here:

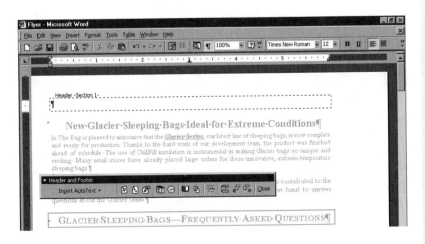

Adding footnotes

Footnotes are used to document sources and to give tangential tidbits of information when their inclusion in the main text would detract from the discussion. To add a footnote, click an insertion point after the word where you want the footnote reference mark to be placed. Then choose Footnote from the Insert menu to display the Footnote And Endnote dialog box. By default, Word automatically numbers footnotes and places them at the bottom of the page. (Click the Endnote option to have your reference appear at the end of your document.) To change the placement of footnotes or endnotes, the number format, or numbering options, click the Options button in the Footnote And Endnote dialog box and make the appropriate adjustments. When you click OK, Word inserts a superscripted 1 (or whatever letter or symbol you have chosen) at the location of the insertion point and moves to the bottom of the page or the end of the document—depending on the option you have chosen—and waits for you to type the footnote/endnote text. (In normal view, the footnote/endnote appears in a separate window with the Footnotes toolbar.) When you finish typing the text, click anywhere outside the footnote if you are in print layout view, or click the Close button on the Footnotes toolbar if you are in normal view. If you want to edit your footnotes, choose Footnotes from the View menu.

The Page Setup button

4. Click the Page Setup button on the Header And Footer toolbar to display the Layout tab of the Page Setup dialog box, shown here:

5. In the Headers And Footers section, select the Different First Page check box and click OK. Word changes the header designation to read *First Page Header - Section 1*.

The Show Next button

6. You're going to leave the first page header blank, so click the Show Next button on the Header And Footer toolbar to move to the next page, which begins section 2.

The Same As Previous button

7. Click the Same As Previous button to toggle it off, thereby telling Word that you want this header to be different from the first one.

The Insert Page Number button

8. Now type *In The Bag*, press the Tab key twice, type *Page* and a space, and click the Insert Page Number button.

More about page numbers

If you want your headers or footers to contain nothing but page numbers, you don't have to create a header or footer. You can have Word perform this chore for you. Choose Page Numbers from the Insert menu and in the Page Numbers dialog box, specify whether the numbers should appear at the top or bottom of the page, how they should be aligned, and if a number should appear on the first page. When you click OK, Word inserts page numbers in the document's header or footer. Whether you add page numbers this way or by clicking the Insert Page Number button on the Header And Footer toolbar, you can format them by clicking the Format button in the Page Numbers dialog box. You can select from five numbering schemes: Arabic numbers (1, 2, 3), lowercase/uppercase letters (a, b, c/ A, B, C), and lowercase/uppercase Roman numerals (i, ii, iii/I, II, III). You can also specify whether to include chapter numbers and select a starting number.

9. Select the entire header, click the Bold and Underline buttons, change the font size to 10, and press Home. The header now looks like this:

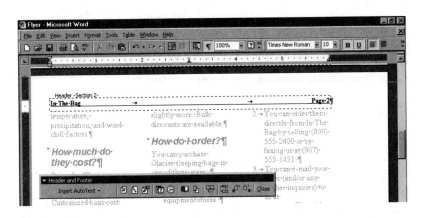

10. Click the Close button on the Header And Footer toolbar to return to print layout view.

Formatting with Styles

You can work through a document applying formats to headings and other special paragraphs one by one, but Word provides an easier way: you can store custom combinations of formatting by defining the combination as a *style*. You can then apply that combination to a text selection or a paragraph simply by selecting the style from the Style drop-down list on the Formatting toolbar.

Every paragraph you write has a style. When you open a new blank document, it is based on the Blank Document template, and Word applies that template's Normal style to all paragraphs unless instructed otherwise. This Normal style formats characters as 12-point regular Times New Roman and paragraphs as left-aligned and single-spaced. When you base a document on a template other than Blank Document, the styles included as part of that template are available, and as you saw earlier in this chapter, you can then create documents like the memo simply by filling in the paragraphs of the template.

The default Normal style

Because you merged the Glacier Memo file with Flyer, the memo's styles have been incorporated into the Flyer document's template. Turn the page to check this out.

1. Click the Formatting toolbar's More Buttons button. Then click the arrow to the right of the Style box to drop down the Style list.

2. Scroll through the list. You'll see that Word has added the styles from the memo template, each displayed in its assigned formatting. Paragraph styles are designated by a paragraph mark and character styles are designated by an *a*.

3. Click a blank area of the document to close the list.

Using Word's Predefined Styles

As you learned in Chapter 2, Word comes with nine predefined heading styles, one for each of the heading levels you can designate when using the Outlining feature. Word also has predefined paragraph styles for a number of other common document elements, such as index entries, headers and footers, and footnotes. For a new document, Word lists only the Heading 1, Heading 2, Heading 3, and Normal paragraph styles and the Default Paragraph Font character style. Word does not list the other predefined styles unless you insert one of those elements in the document. Then Word both applies the corresponding style to the element and adds the style name to the Style list.

When Word applies one of its built-in styles to an element, it uses the formatting that has been predefined for that element. Once the style is available on the Style list, you can apply it to other paragraphs. You can also redefine the style to suit the document you are creating, and you can create new styles.

Creating Custom Styles

Although Word does a good job of anticipating the document elements for which you will need styles, you will often want to come up with styles of your own. Suppose you want to delete the space between the first two paragraphs of the flyer and indent their first lines so that it's easy to tell at a glance where one paragraph ends and the other begins. Follow the steps on the facing page to create a style with this combination of formatting.

Character styles vs. paragraph styles

Character styles affect only the selected text, and these styles are applied on top of any paragraph formats assigned to the selected text. Paragraph styles affect the entire paragraph containing the insertion point. For example, you can apply a paragraph style that makes the font and size of an entire paragraph 12-point regular Arial, and then you can select the first word and apply a character style that makes just that word bold, italic, and underlined. If you later apply a different paragraph style that makes the font and size of the entire paragraph 14-point regular Times New Roman, the first word will remain bold, italic, and underlined.

1. Delete the paragraph mark between the first and second paragraphs.

2. Click an insertion point in the first text paragraph and choose Paragraph from the Format menu to display the dialog box shown here:

3. In the Indentation section, select First Line from the Special drop-down list. Word enters 0.5" in the By edit box as the default first-line indent and shows in the Preview box below how your text will look with this setting.

4. Change the setting in the By edit box to *0.15"*, change the After setting in the Spacing section to *6 pt*, and click OK.

You can assign a different name to the new style by following these steps:

1. With the insertion point located in the first paragraph, click the Formatting toolbar's More Buttons button. Then click the Style box to highlight the style name in it.

2. Type *Indented Paragraph*, the name you want for this style, and then press Enter. Word creates the style, adds its name to the Style list, and displays Indented Paragraph in the Style box to indicate that this style has been applied to the active paragraph.

Line spacing options

At times, you may want to adjust the line spacing in your document. For example, double-spaced text is easier to work with when you are drafting and editing a long document. To change the line spacing, choose Paragraph from the Format menu, and on the Indents And Spacing tab, make your selection from the Line Spacing drop-down list. If you adjust line spacing often, you can create double-spaced versions of your styles and quickly switch to the single-spaced versions when you've finished drafting your document. In addition to the traditional single, 1½, and double-spaced options, you can specify that the line spacing be changed by a certain percentage by selecting the Multiple option. The At Least option ensures that Word will allow enough space for graphics or large font sizes, and the Exactly option makes all lines evenly spaced.

Applying a style

3. Click an insertion point in the second paragraph of the flyer, drop down the Style list, and select the Indented Paragraph style. Word changes the style of the second paragraph so that its formatting is consistent with the first paragraph, like this:

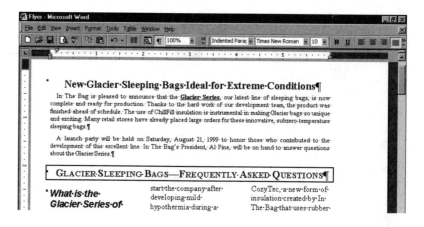

Now turn your attention to the FAQ part of the flyer. Suppose you want to justify these paragraphs and add a little space before each paragraph. (Paragraphs with space before them are called *open paragraphs*.) Follow these steps:

1. Click an insertion point in the first text paragraph of the FAQ section of the flyer, right-click it, and choose Paragraph from the shortcut menu.

The Style dialog box

You can manage all the available styles and also create new ones by choosing Style from the Format menu. You can click the New button to define a new style, the Delete button to remove a selected style, and the Modify button to display a dialog box in which you can change the selected style. You can specify that one style should automatically follow another by selecting the first style, clicking the Modify button, and selecting a style from the Style For Following Paragraph drop-down list.

Modifying styles

To modify one of Word's default styles or one of your own, first select the text that uses the style you want to change and make the necessary formatting changes. Then to redefine the style to include the changes you have made, select it in the Style drop-down list. When Word displays the Modify Style dialog box, select the Update option to modify the existing style, or select the Reapply option to revert to the style's existing formatting. Click the Automatically Update check box if you want the style to be redefined whenever you make a change to text that uses it. (To turn off the Automatically Update option, choose Style from the Format menu, click Modify, deselect the Automatically Update check box, and click OK and then Close.) Click OK to implement your choices, or click Cancel to close the dialog box and leave your formatting changes intact without redefining the style. When you redefine a style, all other occurrences of that style in your current document are updated as well.

2. Select Justified from the Alignment drop-down list in the top left corner of the Paragraph dialog box (the equivalent of clicking the Justify button on the Formatting toolbar). Then in the Spacing section, change the Before setting to *3 pt* and click OK.

3. Select the paragraph, including the paragraph mark, and change the size to 11.

4. Now click the Style box to highlight the name in it, type *Open Paragraph* as this style's name, and press Enter.

5. In turn, select each paragraph of the FAQ (including the numbered paragraphs) and then select Open Paragraph from the Style list to apply that style.

6. Now select the second, third, and fourth paragraphs under the *How do I order?* heading and click the Numbering button on the Formatting toolbar. The numbered-list format is then re-applied on top of the Open Paragraph style.

The Numbering button

Hyphenating Documents

By default, Word does not hyphenate your text, but by hyphenating some words you can really improve the look of the justified skinny columns of the FAQ part of the flyer. Follow these steps:

1. Press Ctrl+Home to move to the top of the document. (You may as well hyphenate all the text.)

2. Choose Language and then Hyphenation from the expanded Tools menu to display the dialog box shown below. (If Word tells you that you need to install this feature, insert the installation CD-ROM if necessary and go ahead.)

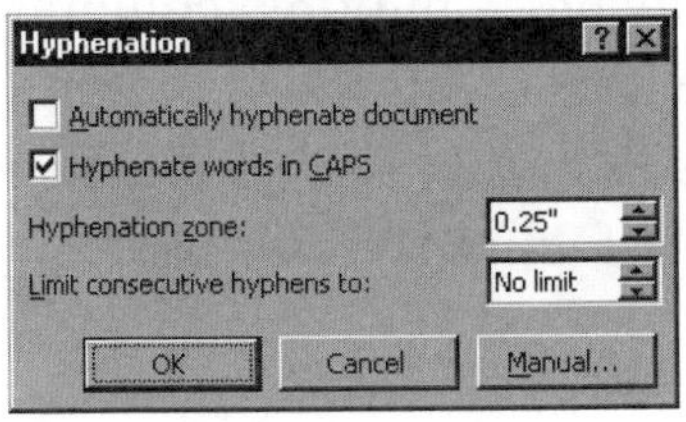

3. Select the Automatically Hyphenate Document check box and click the Hyphenate Words In CAPS check box to deselect it. Then click OK. Word quickly hyphenates the words in the document as needed.

4. Scroll through the flyer, noticing that many of the big spaces between words have disappeared.

In the next section, you'll fix the layout of the pages so that all the text fits on the first page.

Publishing Documents

Whether you are writing a letter, a newsletter, or an annual report, the end product of many of your Word sessions will be a document other people will read, either on paper or via the Internet or your organization's intranet. This section discusses both types of publishing.

If you can print documents on paper from other Windows applications, you should have no trouble printing from Word. If you want to publish your documents as Web pages that can be distributed via the Internet or an intranet, you first have to convert them to *HyperText Markup Language* (HTML) so that they can be viewed in a Web browser program. As you'll see in the following sections, not all Word formatting can be handled by Web browsers, so during conversion, elements such as columns and headers and footers seem to drop out. However, a feature called "round-trip" editing allows you to open a converted HTML document in Word with all the original Word formatting in place. As a result, updating your Web pages is easy to accomplish in Word, and you never have to deal with the underlying HTML coding.

Editing in print preview

Suppose you zoom in on a section of a document and notice something you need to change. To edit the document, click the Magnifier button on the Print Preview toolbar to change the pointer to an insertion point. Make your changes and click the Magnifier button again. Then click the document to zoom out.

Previewing Documents

The flyer is three pages long and includes multiple columns and a header. With all of these elements, you'll want to preview the document to get an idea of how it will look when published. Follow the steps on the facing page to preview the flyer.

1. Click the Print Preview button on the Standard toolbar to display the first page of the flyer as shown here:

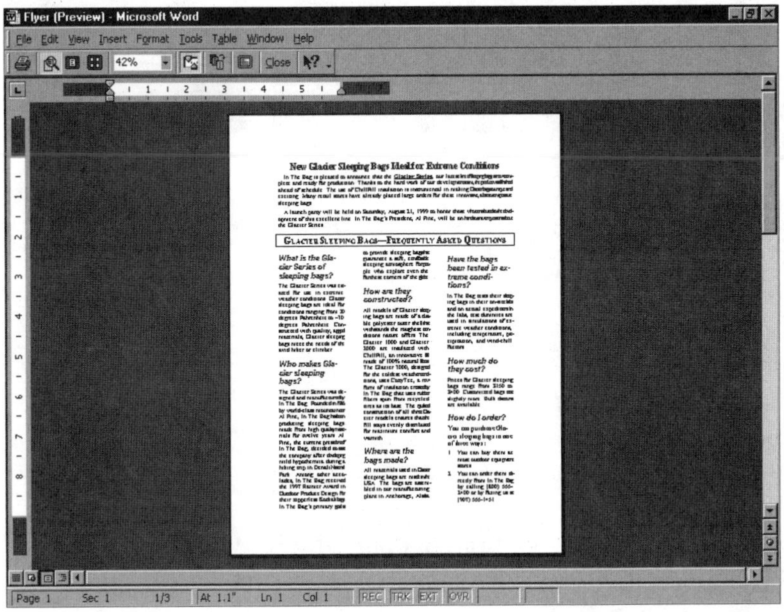

The Print Preview button

2. Move the mouse pointer over the flyer. When the pointer changes to a magnifying glass, click the left mouse button to zoom in on the flyer. Click the mouse button again to zoom out.

Zooming in/out

3. To see more than one page at a time, click the Multiple Pages button on the Print Preview toolbar to drop down a grid of "pages." Point to the left page in the top row, move the pointer over the center page, and click it. Word displays the first two pages of the flyer side by side.

The Multiple Pages button

4. Press the Page Down key to see the third page, and then click the Close button on the Print Preview toolbar.

   Now let's preview how the flyer will look if you publish it as a Web page. (You need to have a Web browser installed on your computer to be able to preview a Web document.) Follow these steps:

1. With Flyer open on your screen, choose Web Page Preview from the File menu. Word makes a temporary copy of the document, codes it with HTML, starts your Web browser, and displays the copy of Flyer as shown on the next page. (We've maximized the browser's window.)

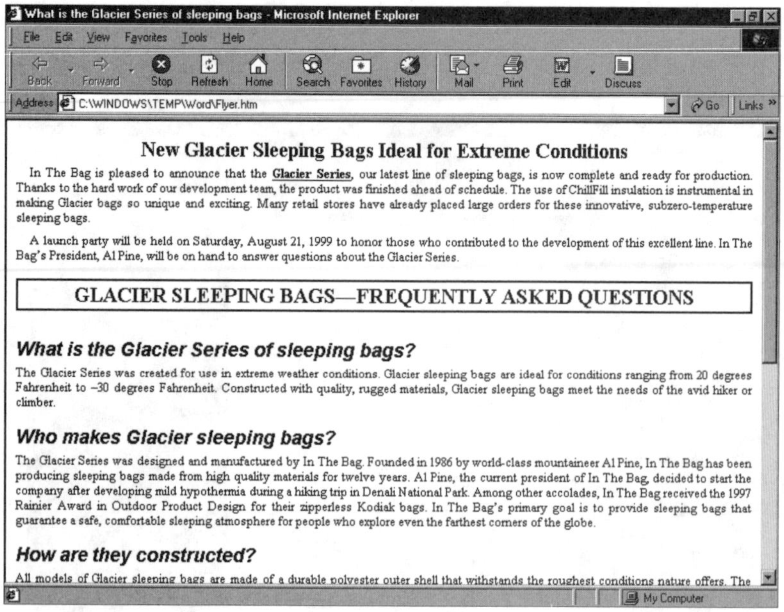

2. Scroll though the Web page, checking how each component has been converted.

3. Click your browser's Close button to exit the program and return to Word.

Changing Page Layout

Let's modify the page layout by changing the bottom margin so that when printed on paper, the text of the flyer fits on one page. Follow these steps:

1. Choose Page Setup from the File menu and if necessary, click the Margins tab to display the dialog box shown here:

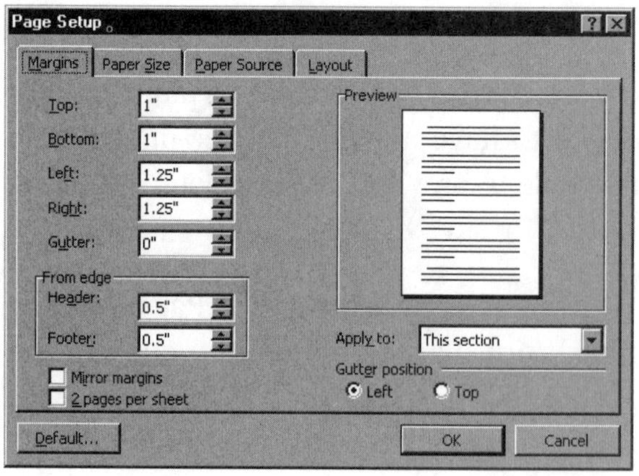

Setting up for printing

When you installed Windows, the Setup program installed the driver (the control program) for a printer attached to your computer or available over your network. To install drivers for other printers, use the Add Printer Wizard in the Printers folder. (Choose Settings and then Printers from the Start menu.) Word can access all the installed printers, but only one at a time. To switch printers, choose Print from the File menu, click the arrow to the right of the Name box in the Printer section, select the printer you want, and click OK.

2. Change the Bottom setting to *0.5"*, the Left setting to *1"*, and the Right setting to *1"*. Then select Whole Document from the Apply To drop-down list, and click OK.

3. Check the document in print preview to verify that all the text now fits on the first page.

4. If you don't like the way any of the headings break, click an insertion point and press Shift+Enter to insert a line break. If you don't like any of the column breaks, click an insertion point and press Ctrl+Shift+Enter.

← Inserting line and column breaks

Printing on Paper

Here's how to print your document:

1. Click the Print button on the Standard toolbar. (You can also print directly from print preview by clicking this button on the Print Preview toolbar.) Voilà! Simple, isn't it?

← The Print button

Word prints the document with the default settings: one copy of the entire document. To print multiple copies or selected pages, you must use the Print command on the File menu instead of the Print button on the toolbar. Follow these steps:

1. Choose Print from the File menu to display this dialog box:

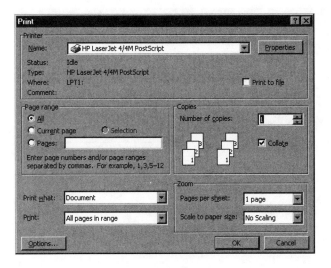

Notice that the Name box tells you which printer Word will use.

2. In the Copies section, type *2* to replace the default setting of 1 in the Number Of Copies edit box.

More printing options

To print selected pages, click the Pages option and then enter the page numbers (for example, *2-4* for pages 2, 3, and 4; and *2,4* for pages 2 and 4 only). In the Print What drop-down list, specify what you want to print. In the Print drop-down list, specify whether you want to print all, all odd, or all even pages. If you don't want Word to collate the pages when printing multiple copies, click the Collate check box to deselect it. Click the Print To File check box to "print" an image of the document to a file on disk. Clicking Properties displays a tabbed dialog box with more printing options. You can print several small pages on one piece of paper in such a way that the paper can be folded to produce booklets of two or four pages. You can also change the page orientation from Portrait (vertical) to Landscape (horizontal).

3. Click the Current Page option in the Page Range section to tell Word to print only the page containing the insertion point.

4. You aren't actually going to print using these specifications, so click Cancel to close the Print dialog box.

Creating a Web Document

With Word's Web publishing tools, you can easily create a great-looking Web page from scratch (see the tip below) or convert an existing document into a Web page without any prior knowledge of HTML. Here, we'll take a look at how to convert an existing file to HTML format so that it can be viewed on the Internet or on an intranet. Let's get started:

Saving an existing document in Web format

1. Choose Save As Web Page from the File menu to display a dialog box similar to the Save As dialog box shown earlier on page 21. Type *Web Flyer* as the name and click Save to store this version of the document in the My Documents folder on your hard drive. (See the tip on the facing page for information about storing HTML files on a Web server.)

2. If Word tells you it can't convert some of the flyer's features to HTML, click Continue. Word then displays Web Flyer in web layout view, like this:

Using the Web Page Wizard

If you want to create a personal or business Web site for the Internet or an intranet, an easy way to get started is to use the Web Page Wizard. Choose New from the File menu, click the Web Pages tab, and double-click the Web Page Wizard icon. Then in the wizard's dialog boxes, select the type and style of page you want to create. After the wizard creates the page, you can insert your information and edit and format it without having to know the ins and outs of HTML coding.

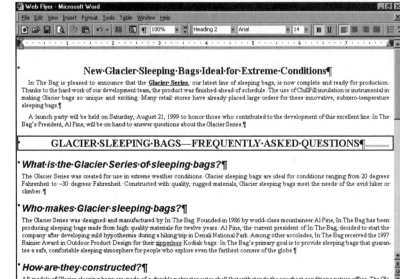

As you can see, the flyer looks pretty much as it did when displayed in web preview.

Formatting Web Documents

Once you have converted a document to a Web page, you will probably want to apply formatting that is supported by Web browsers to jazz it up. Let's add some horizontal lines, change the background texture, and change the font color:

1. Click an insertion point at the beginning of the first text paragraph in the flyer (after the heading) and then choose Borders And Shading from the Format menu to display the dialog box shown earlier on page 69.

Adding horizontal lines

2. On the Borders tab, click the Horizontal Line button to display this version of the Clip Gallery dialog box:

Here you can select from many horizontal line designs. When you click a design, Word displays a menu of buttons for previewing the line, inserting it, adding the line to your list of favorites, and finding other similar line designs. (For information about the other options in this window, ask the Office Assistant to search for the Clip Gallery topic in Word's Help feature.)

Saving on a Web server

To save a file on a Web server, click the Web Folders icon in the Save As dialog box to display the locations that are available to you. Select the Web location you want to use and then click Save. To set up the Web locations so that they can be accessed from the Web Folders icon, open Windows Explorer and click Web Folders. Next double-click Add Web Folder to work through a series of dialog boxes that help you specify the URL of the Web location you want to add.

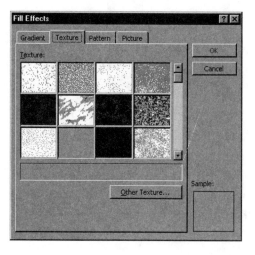

The Insert Clip button

3. Click the first style in the third row and click the Insert Clip button to insert a horizontal line that separates the paragraph from the title above, as shown here:

Now let's change the background and font color of the flyer:

Changing the page background

1. Press Ctrl+Home to move to the top of the page, and choose Background and then Fill Effects from the Format menu to display the Fill Effects dialog box.

2. Click the Texture tab to display these options:

Web page themes

You can apply a coordinated design to the Web pages you create. Choose Themes from the Format menu, select a theme in the list on the left to view its main components in the pane on the right, and click OK when you find an appropriate design.

3. Click the third option in the first row and click OK to apply that texture to the background of the flyer.

4. Press Ctrl+A to select all the flyer's text, click the arrow to the right of the Font Color button on the Formatting toolbar, and select Dark Red in the second row of the palette.

The Font Color button

5. Click anywhere to remove the highlighting and view the results shown here:

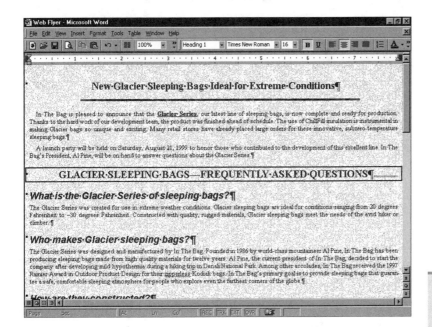

6. Save your changes.

Inserting Hyperlinks

You may want to add hyperlinks to your Web documents so that viewers can move to related pages. Hyperlinks are often used for other Web site addresses or e-mail addresses. However, they also have other uses. For example, if a Web document references a particular budget spreadsheet, you can create a hyperlink to the spreadsheet so that viewers can move immediately to the spreadsheet file. (See the adjacent tip for more information.) As a demonstration, you will add a hyperlink to In The Bag's e-mail address. Follow the steps on the next page.

Creating hyperlinks to files

To turn text in your Web page into a hyperlink to a specific file, select the text and click the Insert Hyperlink button on the Standard toolbar. In the Link To bar, check that Existing File Or Web Page is selected, type the path of the file or click the File or Web Page button in the Browse For section to navigate to the file's location. Then click OK. When you click the hyperlink, the originating program starts, opens the file, and displays the Web toolbar. Click the Back button on the Web toolbar to return to the Web page. (For information about the Web toolbar, see the tip on page 88.)

1. Select the e-mail address in the last paragraph of the flyer and choose Hyperlink from the Insert menu. In the Insert Hyperlink dialog box, click the E-Mail Address icon on the Link To bar to display these options:

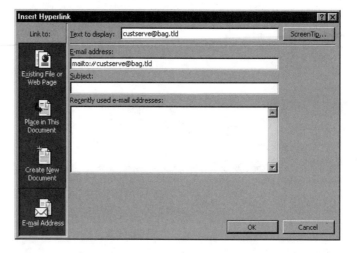

2. If the Text To Display and E-Mail Address edit boxes don't contain these entries, adjust them to look as shown above (edit first the E-Mail Address box and then the Text To Display box), and click OK. Word formats the selected text as a hyperlink by changing the text color to light blue and underlining it. (When creating a Web page from scratch, you can type an e-mail address, and Word will automatically create the hyperlink for you.)

Viewing the HTML source

If you know HTML, you can edit the code and text by choosing the HTML Source command from Word's View menu. Word then loads the Microsoft Development Environment program in a separate window, which displays the HTML coding of your Web page. When you finish editing, choose Exit from the File menu to return to the formatted version of the document in Word.

The Web toolbar

When you click a hyperlink in a Word document, Word displays the Web toolbar, which you can use to easily access the Internet or your intranet. (You can also display it by right-clicking any displayed toolbar and choosing Web from the toolbar's shortcut menu.) You can use the Back and Forward buttons to move back and forth through recently opened documents or Web pages. If you want to mark a page as a favorite so that you can easily access it later, display the page, click the Favorites button on the Web toolbar, choose Add To Favorites, and then click Add. To open that page later, click the arrow to the right of the Favorites button to display your Favorites list and select the page from the bottom of the list. To search the Web, click the Search The Web button. If you want to move directly to a file or Web page, simply type in the path or address in the Address box and press Enter to jump to the file or page.

3. Before you publish your Web page, preview it in your Web browser to make sure that everything looks OK. Here's what the hyperlink looks like:

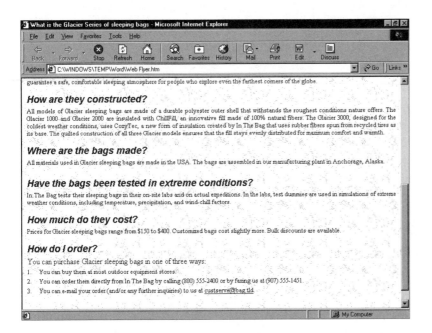

4. Save and close Web Flyer and exit Word.

   Obviously, the Web page you have created is very simple, and it could be dramatically enhanced with graphics, colors, background images, video, and other elements. (Bear in mind though that these elements can dramatically increase the download time of your Web pages.) We will leave it up to you to explore on your own if you want to know more about creating Web pages.

TWO

BUILDING PROFICIENCY

In Part Two, you build on the skills from Part One while creating more complex documents. In Chapter 4, you create and format tables, and then learn how to use forms to save valuable time. In Chapter 5, you design templates and incorporate fancy text and graphics to liven up your documents. Then you add a graph and a spreadsheet to display data. Finally, in Chapter 6, you use mail merge to print simple and complex form letters and mailing labels. After completing this book, you'll be able to create most types of professional documents.

Tables and Forms

4

Tables and forms lend structure and organization to information in your Word documents. In this chapter, you use tabs to create simple tabular lists. Then you create and format more complex tables using Word's tables feature. Finally, you create and fill in a simple form.

You use tables first to display In The Bag's monthly sales figures, and then to create a letterhead for the company. You can also use tables to create invoices or purchase orders for your business or organization.

Documents created and concepts covered:

Set tabs to create a simple tabular list

Create and format tables visually

Dear Cliff:

Here is the information you requested:

Style	Weight	Base Price
Glacier 1000	3 lb. 9 oz.	$140.00
Glacier 2000	4 lb. 11 oz.	$225.50
Glacier 3000	5 lb. 9 oz.	$325.50

GLACIER SLEEPING BAGS GROSS SALES			
July-December 1999			
Month	Glacier 1000	Glacier 2000	Glacier 3000
July	$35,100.10	$45,500.45	$57,800.30
August	$32,450.40	$42,400.65	$52,000.00
September	$40,600.00	$61,250.30	$68,520.65
October	$52,700.65	$70,320.00	$89,630.85
November	$67,350.80		
December	$102,000.90		
TOTAL	$330,202.85		
AVERAGE	$55,033.81		

Call me if you have any questions.

Ida Down

Design a professional-looking header using the Insert Table button

IN THE BAG
Business
Travel
Expenses

Reason for Travel:

Airfare:	**Payment Method:**	Corporate CC
Meals:	**Payment Method:**	Personal CC
Hotel:	**Payment Method:**	Corporate CC

Miscellaneous (Cash):

Mileage:	
Parking:	
Tolls:	
Taxis:	
TOTAL:	$0.00

Perform calculations with formulas

Use the Forms toolbar to set up a business form template

I n the interests of clarity, you will want to display certain types of information in a table rather than in a narrative paragraph. In a table, individual items are easier to spot, and relationships between items are more obvious. With Word, you can use tabs to create simple tables, or you can design more complex and flexible tables using Word's tables feature. We cover both methods in this chapter. We also teach you how to set up forms. Like tables, forms lend a structure to information, but their purpose is different. You use forms to facilitate the input of information rather than simply display it.

Creating Tabular Lists

For simple tables, you can set tabs so that you can align information neatly in columns. This type of table is known as a *tabular list*. Follow these steps to create a tabular list now:

1. With Word loaded and a blank document on your screen, check that you are in print layout view and that the rulers and nonprinting characters are turned on. (We've reduced the magnification of our screen to see more information at one time.)

2. Type the following:

   Dear Cliff: (Press Enter twice)
   Here is the information you requested: (Press Enter twice)

3. Type *Style* and press Tab. The insertion point jumps to a position on the screen that corresponds to that of the next tab setting, which is indicated by a tiny line on the gray bar below the ruler.

4. Type *Weight*, press Tab, type *Base Price*, and press Enter to end the first line of the list.

5. Choose Save As from the File menu, type *Sales Memo* as the filename, and then press Enter or click Save.

6. Now type the following, pressing Tab where indicated by the ➡ and pressing Enter at the end of each line:

Glacier 1000	➡	*3 lb. 9 oz.*	➡	*$140.00*
Glacier 2000	➡	*4 lb. 11 oz.*	➡	*$225.50*
Glacier 3000	➡	*5 lb. 9 oz.*	➡	*$325.50*

Setting tabs with the Tabs command

Instead of using the ruler, you can choose Tabs from the Format menu to display a dialog box in which you can set tabs. Enter the tab position in the Tab Stop Position edit box and click Set. Word adds the tab to the Tab Stop Position list below the edit box. You can specify how the text should be aligned at the tab and whether the tabs should have leaders. For example, if you create a table of contents for a report, you might want to set a right tab with dot leaders to draw your readers' eyes from the headings across the page to the page numbers.

You need to adjust the tab settings to align the sleeping-bag information with the headings, but first let's indent the entire list. (As a general rule, you should always apply all other formatting, including character formatting, to a list before setting tabs, because the slightest change can make the text columns jump annoyingly out of alignment.) Try this:

1. Select the four lines of the tabular list and click the Increase Indent button on the Formatting toolbar. Word indents the selected text to the first tab setting, as shown here:

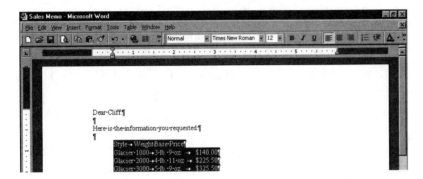

The Increase Indent button

On the ruler, two triangular markers now sit on a small rectangular marker at the ½-inch mark. The top triangle controls how much the first line of the active paragraph is indented, and the bottom triangle controls how much the rest of the paragraph is indented. You can adjust the first-line or paragraph indent by manually dragging the corresponding triangle, or you can adjust both at once by dragging the rectangle.

2. With the tabular list still selected, point to the rectangle at the ½-inch mark on the ruler, hold down the mouse button, and drag the rectangle to the left to the second tick mark (the ¼-inch mark). The two triangles move with the rectangle. When you release the mouse button, Word adjusts the indent for the entire list.

Adjusting indents with the ruler

Now let's align the columns so that the items in the second, third, and fourth rows align with their column headers. You need to set tabs so that the lines in the second column align at 1½ inches and those in the third column align at 3¼ inches. Follow the steps on the next page.

Default tab settings

By default, Word sets tabs every ½ inch across the page. You can adjust their position by choosing Tabs from the Format menu and changing the Default Tab Stops setting. When you set a custom tab, Word removes all the default tabs to the left of the new tab but retains the default tabs to the right.

1. Without moving the selection, point to the 1½-inch mark on the ruler and click the left mouse button once. A left-aligned tab marker (an *L*) appears on the ruler, and the items in the second column of all the selected lines jump to left-align themselves at that position on the screen.

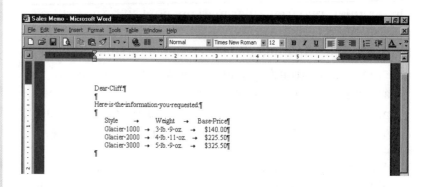

The Tab button

2. Click the Tab button at the left end of the ruler. The icon on the button changes to indicate that clicking the ruler now will set a centered tab (an upside-down *T*), which would cause all the items in the column to center themselves on the tab's position.

3. Click the Tab button again to activate a right-aligned tab (a backwards *L*), and then click the ruler at the 3¼-inch mark. The items in the third column of the selected lines jump to right-align themselves at that position. (Clicking the Tab button again would activate a decimal-aligned tab, which you can use to align numbers on their decimal points; see page 102.)

4. Press Ctrl+End to remove the highlight and move to the end of the memo, which now looks like the one shown here:

5. Press Enter once to add a blank line, and type *Call me if you have any questions*. Then press Enter four times and type *Ida Down*.

6. Save the memo. (Save frequently from now on.)

Creating Tables

As we said earlier, tables provide visual summaries of information and enable you to quickly grasp relationships that might be lost in narrative explanations. Creating tables in Word is a simple process. You specify the number of columns and rows

---

Other ways to create tables

You can create a table with specific column widths by choosing Insert and then Table from the Table menu and entering specifications in the Insert Table dialog box. From this dialog box, you can also move to the Table AutoFormat dialog box (see the tip on page 103). Yet another way to create a table is to use the Draw Table button on the Tables And Borders toolbar. Click the button to activate the drawing tool (the pointer turns into a pencil) and drag it diagonally to draw a box. When the box is the size you want the table to be, release the mouse button. Next draw horizontal and vertical lines to create rows and columns. To remove a line, simply click the Eraser button on the Tables And Borders toolbar to activate the Eraser tool and click the line you want to erase. You can erase one border of a cell to merge cells either vertically or horizontally. To turn off either the Draw Table or Eraser tool, click the appropriate button to toggle it off. You can then edit and format the table just as you would any other table.

and then leave it to Word to figure out the initial settings. To demonstrate how easy the process is, let's add a table to the memo you just created:

1. Click an insertion point to the left of the *C* in *Call* and then press Enter.

2. Press the Up Arrow key to move back to the empty paragraph you just inserted, and then click the Insert Table button on the Standard toolbar to drop down a column/row grid.

The Insert Table button

3. Point to the top left square, hold down the left mouse button, and drag the pointer across four columns and down seven rows. The grid expands as you drag beyond its bottom edge, and Word shows the size of the selection below the grid. When you release the mouse button, Word inserts a table structure in the document like the one shown here:

As you can see, Word has created a table with four equal columns, and the table automatically spans the width of the document's text column. The insertion point is in the table's first *cell* (the intersection of the first column and the first row). To make an entry in this cell, all you have to do is type. Follow these steps:

1. To enter column headings, type *Month* in the first cell and press Tab. The insertion point moves to the cell to the right.

Deleting/inserting rows and columns

To delete one or more rows or columns, select them and choose Delete and then Rows or Columns from the Table menu. (If you choose Delete and then Cells, Word displays a dialog box where you can specify what you want to delete.) To delete the entire table, select it and choose Delete and then Table from the Table menu. If you press the Delete key to accomplish any of these tasks, the contents of the cells are deleted but not the cells themselves. To insert rows or columns, select the number of rows or columns you want to add. Next choose Insert and then Rows Above or Rows Below or Columns To The Left or Columns To The Right from the Table menu. You can also use the Insert Rows or Insert Columns button on the Standard toolbar (see page 101).

2. Type *Glacier 3000* and press Tab to move to the next cell. Next type *Glacier 2000*, press Tab, type *Glacier 1000*, and press Tab. Notice that pressing Tab at the end of the first row moves the insertion point to the first cell in the second row.

3. Finish the table by typing the entries shown below, pressing Tab to move from cell to cell. (Pressing Shift+Tab moves the insertion point to the previous cell, and you can also use the Arrow keys and the mouse to move around.)

Moving around a table

July	*$57,800.30*	*$45,500.45*	*$35,100.10*
August	*$52,000.00*	*$42,400.65*	*$32,450.40*
September	*$68,520.65*	*$61,250.30*	*$40,600.00*
October	*$89,630.85*	*$70,320.00*	*$52,700.65*
November	*$102,960.90*	*$89,850.50*	*$67,350.80*
December	*$119,320.75*	*$106,950.40*	*$102,000.90*

Here are the results so far:

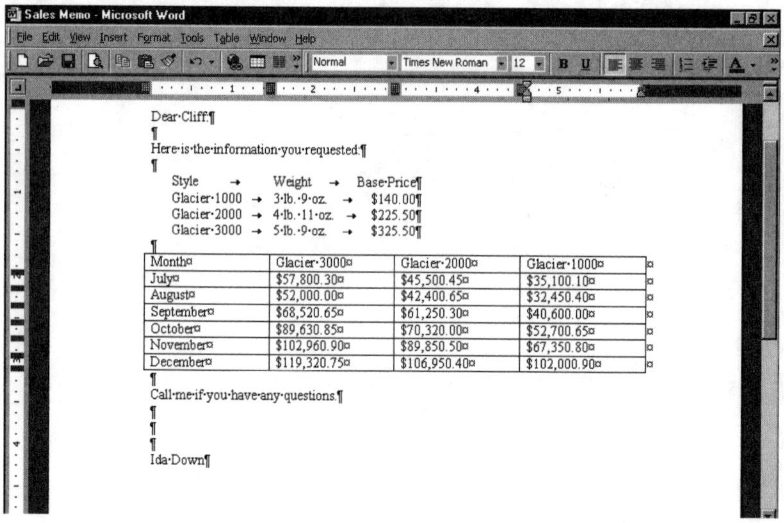

Looking over the table, you can probably see one or two changes that would make it more effective. We discuss ways to edit tables in the next section.

Rearranging Tables

You can rearrange the rows and columns in a table in much the same way that you rearrange text. Let's switch the Glacier 3000 column with the Glacier 1000 column:

1. Click any cell in the Glacier 1000 column and choose Select and then Column from the Table menu. (You can choose Select and then Row to select the row containing the active cell, or Select and then Table to select the entire table.)

Selecting a column

2. Point to the selected column, hold down the mouse button, drag the shadow insertion point to the beginning of the Glacier 3000 heading, and release the mouse button. The Glacier 1000 column moves to the left of the Glacier 3000 column.

Moving a column

3. Now select the Glacier 2000 column and move it to the left of the Glacier 3000 column. The results are shown here:

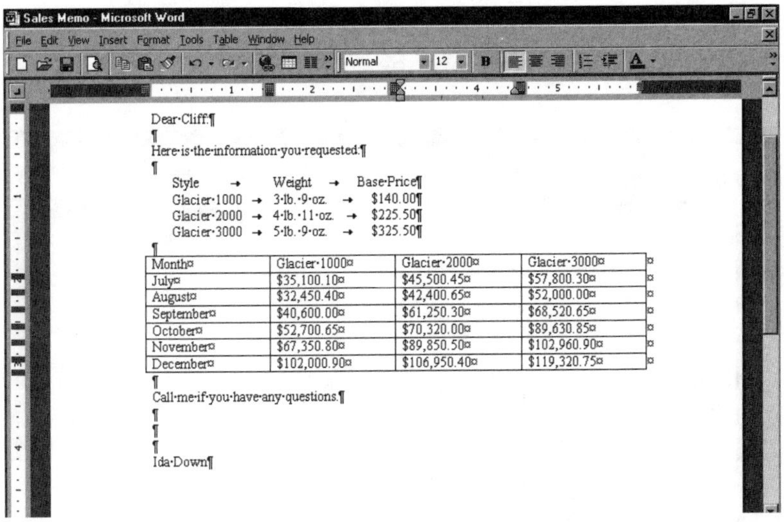

Changing Column Width

You can adjust column widths in three ways: by moving the column markers designated with grids on the ruler, by dragging column borders, or by using the Table Properties command. Follow these steps to change the widths of the columns in the sample table:

1. With the insertion point located anywhere in the table, move the pointer over the grid at the left end of the active part of the horizontal ruler. When the pointer changes to a two-headed arrow with a ScreenTip that reads *Move Table Column*, hold down the left mouse button and drag to the right until the first column of the table is aligned with the text in the first column

Resizing rows

In print layout view, you can manually adjust the size of table rows. Simply move the pointer over the row's bottom border and drag up or down to the desired size. If you hold down the Alt key as you drag, Word displays the exact row height in the adjacent vertical ruler. (You can also drag the gray bars in the vertical ruler to adjust row height.)

of the tabular list above. (This can be tricky. If the table jumps too far, click the Undo button and try again.)

Changing column widths with the ruler

2. Next point to the column marker on the ruler between the first and second columns and drag the marker to the left until the first column is just wide enough for its entries. Then drag the column marker between the second and third columns to adjust the width of the second column to hold its entries.

3. Now adjust the third and fourth columns using a different method. First point to the right border of any cell in the third column, and then drag the two-headed arrow to the left to about the 3¼-inch mark on the ruler. Repeat this procedure for the fourth column so that the right edge of the table ends at the 4¼-inch mark. Here are the results:

Word wrapping in tables

By default, Word wraps long entries to the number of lines necessary to show the entries in their entirety, adjusting the height of the row as needed. To show all entries on one line, select the row, choose Table Properties from the Table menu, click the Row tab, and click Specify Height. Then select Exactly from the Row Height Is drop-down list, enter the height, and click OK.

Moving tables

You can move a table anywhere in your document. First click an insertion point in the table to select it. When Word displays a framed four-headed arrow outside the top left corner of the table, point to it, hold down the left mouse button, and drag the table to the desired location. (As you drag, Word displays a dotted frame indicating where the table will appear when you release the mouse button.) To modify the way text flows around the table, check that the table is still selected and then choose Table Properties from the Table menu. On the Table tab, select the desired alignment option and click OK. To fine-tune the positioning even further, you can click the Positioning button on the Table tab and enter measurements such as the distance of the table from the surrounding text.

Adding a Title

Suppose you want to add a row above the table to contain a title. The first step is to insert a new row:

1. Move the pointer into the invisible selection bar adjacent to the first row of the table, and click to select the entire row. Or click any of the cells in the top row and choose Select and then Row from the Table menu.

2. Now click the Insert Rows button on the Standard toolbar. Word inserts the number of rows you have selected—in this case, just one.

The Insert Rows button

Next you need to join the cells of the new row to create one large cell to accommodate the table's title. Joining cells is a simple procedure, as you'll see as you follow these steps:

1. Click the Tables And Borders button on the Standard toolbar to display the Tables And Borders toolbar, and then dock the toolbar below the Standard and Formatting toolbars. (See page 12 for information about docking toolbars.)

2. With the first row of the table selected, click the Merge Cells button on the Tables And Borders toolbar. Word combines the cells into one large cell that spans the table.

The Merge Cells button

Sorting tables

You can use the Sort Ascending and Sort Descending buttons on the Tables And Borders toolbar to sort the information in a table. First select the column containing the information you want to sort by—for example, you might sort a table of membership information by name, date, or type of membership. Then click the Sort Ascending button to sort starting with A (or the lowest digit), or click the Sort Descending button to sort starting with Z (or the highest digit). For more complex sorts, click an insertion point anywhere in the table and choose Sort from the Table menu. In the Sort dialog box, you can designate up to three columns to sort by—for example, you might sort the membership information first by type, then by date, and then by name.

Printing headings

If a table is longer than one page, you can instruct Word to print the table headings at the top of all pages on which the table appears. Select the row(s) containing the headings and choose Heading Rows Repeat from the Table menu. To turn off this feature, click an insertion point in the original heading row(s) and again choose Heading Rows Repeat from the Table menu.

3. Now enter the title. Click an insertion point in the top row, type *GLACIER SLEEPING BAGS GROSS SALES*, press Enter, and type *July-December 1999*. Here are the results:

Formatting Tables

Having made all the necessary structural changes to the table, let's add some finishing touches. First you'll format the title and headings:

1. Select the first two rows of the table, click the Center button, and then press Home to remove the highlighting and see the results.

2. To make the table title and the headings in the *Month* column bold, point to the left of the word *GLACIER* in the title, hold down the mouse button, and drag downward through the first column. Then click the Bold button.

Well, that was simple. Now let's see how to decimal-align the numbers in the second, third, and fourth columns. This involves setting decimal tabs in each of these columns. Follow these steps:

Setting a decimal tab

1. Click the Tab button at the left end of the ruler until it is set to a decimal tab (an upside-down *T* with a period).

2. To align the numbers in the Glacier 1000 column on the decimal point, drag through the six cells containing numbers in that column to select them. Then click the $1^5/_8$-inch mark on the ruler (see the graphic below) to set a decimal tab where you want the decimal points to line up.

3. Repeat the previous step to decimal-align the Glacier 2000 and Glacier 3000 numbers in their columns. Click to remove the highlighting and see the results, which look like this:

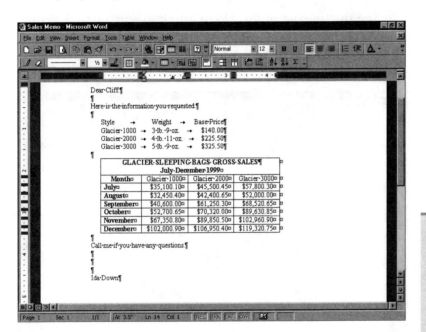

4. Before you move on, save the memo.

   By default, Word puts a ½-pt single-line gridline around each cell and a ½-pt single-line border around the whole table. Before we wrap up this section, let's experiment with gridlines and table borders:

1. With the insertion point anywhere in the table, choose Select and then Table from the Table menu.

2. Click the arrow to the right of the Line Weight box on the Tables And Borders toolbar and then select ¾ pt from the drop-down list.

Table autoformats

An easy way to apply formatting to a table is to use Word's table autoformats. Simply click an insertion point in the table you want to format and click the Table AutoFormat button located on the Tables And Borders toolbar, or choose Table AutoFormat from the Table menu. In the Table AutoFormat dialog box, you can choose from a variety of table styles. Click a name in the Formats list, and Word will display a sample of the format in the Preview box. You can then modify the style using the options in the lower portion of the dialog box. Click OK to complete the changes, and you instantly have a great-looking table. To remove an autoformat, simply choose None from the Formats list.

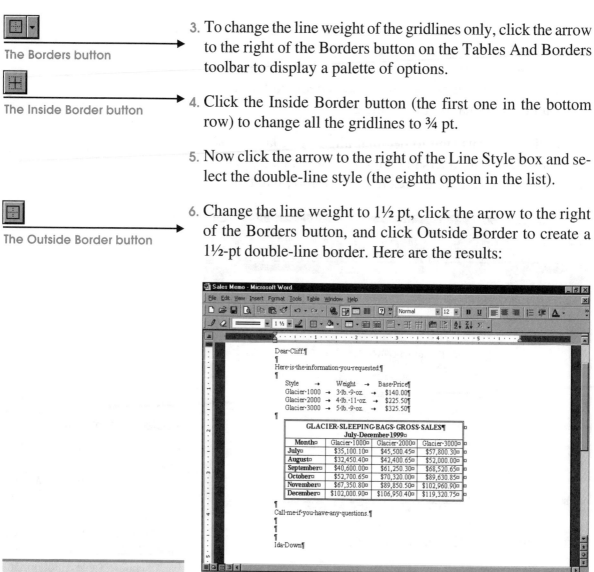

The Borders button

The Inside Border button

The Outside Border button

3. To change the line weight of the gridlines only, click the arrow to the right of the Borders button on the Tables And Borders toolbar to display a palette of options.

4. Click the Inside Border button (the first one in the bottom row) to change all the gridlines to ¾ pt.

5. Now click the arrow to the right of the Line Style box and select the double-line style (the eighth option in the list).

6. Change the line weight to 1½ pt, click the arrow to the right of the Borders button, and click Outside Border to create a 1½-pt double-line border. Here are the results:

7. Save your work.

Calculations in Tables

In Chapter 5, we demonstrate how to import a spreadsheet into Word (see page 145), but Word includes a variety of functions that you can use to build formulas directly in Word tables. Let's add a totals row to the gross sales table and see how easily you can turn a Word table into a simple "spreadsheet." Follow the steps on the facing page.

Turning off gridlines

By default, Word gives tables a border and gridlines. If you want a table without a border or gridlines, select the table, click the Borders button on the Tables And Borders toolbar, and then click the No Border button. To display gridlines that won't print but help you manipulate the structure of the table, choose Show Gridlines from the Table menu. Choose Hide Gridlines to turn them back off.

1. To add a row to the bottom of the table, click an insertion point to the right of the entry in the table's last cell (just before the end-of-cell marker) and press Tab.

Adding a row to the
bottom of a table

2. In the first column of the new row, type *TOTAL* and then press Tab to move to the next column.

The AutoSum button

3. Click the AutoSum button on the Tables And Borders toolbar. Word quickly looks above the selected cell and calculates the sum of the values entered in the cells above.

4. Press Tab to move to the next column.

5. Click the AutoSum button again to total the current column of values.

6. Repeat step 5 for the final column. Your table now looks like this one:

GLACIER SLEEPING BAGS GROSS SALES			
July-December 1999			
Month	Glacier 1000	Glacier 2000	Glacier 3000
July	$35,100.10	$45,500.45	$57,800.30
August	$32,450.40	$42,400.65	$52,000.00
September	$40,600.00	$61,250.30	$68,520.65
October	$52,700.65	$70,320.00	$89,630.85
November	$67,350.80	$89,850.50	$102,960.90
December	$102,000.90	$106,950.40	$119,320.75
TOTAL	$330,202.85	$416,272.30	$490,233.45

7. Do your results include the numbers in the headings (1000, 2000, and 3000)? If your results are incorrect, use the Formula command on the Table menu and follow steps 2 through 5 in the next example, using the SUM function and precise cell specifications to total the values.

Caution!

Let's see how to average the gross sales:

Using the AVERAGE function → 1. Add a row to the bottom of the table, type *AVERAGE* in the first column of the new row and press Tab. (If the column is too narrow to accommodate the word *AVERAGE*, Word automatically adjusts the width of the column.)

2. Choose Formula from the Table menu to display the dialog box shown here:

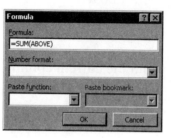

3. Select the contents of the Formula edit box, and press Delete to erase the default entry.

4. Type an = sign, and then click the arrow to the right of the Paste Function edit box to display a list of functions. Click AVERAGE. Word pastes the function and a set of parentheses in the Formula edit box.

5. The numbers you want to average are in the second column—column B—and in rows 3 through 8 of the table, so type *B3:B8* between the parentheses, and click OK.

Totaling cells to the left

If your table is structured so that the values you want to total are oriented from left to right instead of top to bottom, you can click the AutoSum button for the first row you want to total. For the remaining rows, however, choose Formula from the Table menu, then change the =SUM(ABOVE) formula in the Formula edit box to =SUM(LEFT), and click OK.

Specifying number formats

When using the Formula dialog box to create formulas in your Word tables, you can specify a number format for the result of the formula, such as currency or a percentage. To specify a number format, display the Formula dialog box, click the arrow to the right of the Number Format edit box, select the format you want, and click OK.

Updating calculations

After adding a formula to a Word table, you may need to update the formula if you change the data or add/delete a row. Simply select the cell containing the formula and press the F9 key. If the formula references specific cells, such as the AVERAGE formula in our example, you must open the Formula dialog box and adjust the cell references manually to update the calculation.

6. Repeat steps 2 through 5 for the other two columns, using C3:C8 and D3:D8 as the cell specifications.

7. Save the memo, print it, and then close the document.

You might want to take some time to explore Word's functions on your own. They may not let you create sophisticated stock projections or loan analyses, but if your spreadsheet formulas usually involve nothing more complex than a few mathematical calculations, being able to create spreadsheets in Word may save you considerable time.

When Is a Table Not a Table?

Sometimes you can use Word's tables feature to create elements of a document not normally thought of as "tables." For example, a table can be used to create a letterhead or fax cover sheet form. By using the table structure, you can more easily manipulate blocks of text that appear side by side, because they are contained in different cells of the table.

In this section, you'll create a simple header for a business travel expense form. Follow these steps to see how easy it is to use this technique to create a letterhead using Word's tables feature:

1. Click the New button on the Standard toolbar to open a new, blank document.

2. Next click the Insert Table button and then drag across two columns and one row.

3. In the table's first cell, type *IN THE BAG*. Press Tab and type *Business Travel Expenses*.

4. Save the document as *Travel Expenses Form*.

The header doesn't look like much yet, so let's add some formatting to jazz it up a bit. Follow these steps:

1. Click to the left of the text in the first cell to select it, and then change the font to 48-point, bold Arial.

Turning a table into text and vice versa

To convert a table to tabular text, select the entire table and choose Convert and then Table To Text from the Table menu. Indicate how you want Word to separate the information that's now in columns and click OK. Word removes the table grid and separates the text that was in columns as you indicated. To turn a block of regular text separated by tabs into a table, select all the tabular text and click the Insert Table button on the toolbar. If the text is separated by characters other than tabs, select the text, choose Convert and then Text To Table from the Table menu, indicate the number of columns and how the information is separated, and then click OK. You can also click the Draw Table button on the Tables And Borders toolbar and drag the Draw Table tool diagonally across tabular text to convert it to a table.

The Shading Color button

2. To make the text white and the background black, first click the arrow to the right of the Shading Color button on the Tables And Borders toolbar to display a color palette.

3. Click Black (the first option in the fourth row). Word changes the background to black, although you cannot see this effect because your text is still selected.

Changing font color

4. Without moving the selection, choose Font from the Format menu. Click the arrow to the right of the Font Color edit box and select White. Then click the Small Caps check box in the Effects section.

Changing character spacing

5. Now click the Character Spacing tab and click the arrow to the right of the Spacing edit box. Select Expanded and in the By edit box, change the setting to *7.5 pt* to increase the space between characters. Click OK and then click anywhere in the document. The header looks like this:

Now quickly format the second column of the header:

1. Select the text in the second cell and then change its font to 14-point Times New Roman.

The Cell Alignment button

2. To shift the text down in the cell so that it aligns better visually with the first cell, click the arrow to the right of the Cell Alignment button on the Tables And Borders toolbar and select Align Center Left.

Now adjust the column widths:

1. Click the first column, choose Table Properties from the Table menu, and click the Column tab to see these options:

2. Change the Preferred Width setting to 5.1, click the Next Column button, and change the Preferred Width setting to 1. Then click OK. Press Ctrl+End to see these results:

3. Turn off the Tables And Borders toolbar by clicking the Tables And Borders button. Then save the document, which you will use in the next section when you create a form.

Creating Forms

So far, you have used tabular lists and tables to display certain types of information in an organized manner. You could create invoices, purchase orders, or similar documents using these techniques, but there's an easier way. You can create a document called a *form* and then press the Tab key to skip over the text entries that don't change, which are called *labels*, and jump to the areas that need to be filled in, which are called *form fields*.

More text-alignment tools for tables

In addition to the many options available when you click the Cell Alignment button, several other text-alignment buttons are available on the Tables And Borders toolbar. For example, you can rotate the text within its cell by clicking the Change Text Direction button. To return the text in a cell to its default setting, select the cell, rotate it so that its text reads from left to right, click the Cell Alignment button, and select Align Top Left.

To see how to create forms, let's design a business travel expenses form for In The Bag. Follow these steps:

1. With the insertion point at the bottom of Travel Expenses Form, press Enter a couple of times to add some space between the header and the form you are about to create.

2. Right-click any toolbar, choose Forms from the shortcut menu, and then dock the Forms toolbar below the Standard and Formatting toolbars.

Here's how to create form fields using the toolbar buttons:

1. Type *Reason for Travel:* and press Tab. Click the Text Form Field button. Word inserts the field at the insertion point:

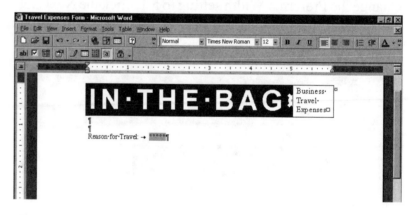

2. Press Enter to start a new line, type *Airfare:*, and press Tab.

3. Click the Text Form Field button and then click the Form Field Options button to display this dialog box:

4. Click the arrow to the right of the Type box and select Number. Next click the arrow to the right of the Number Format

edit box and select the fifth option (the one that contains dollar signs). Then click OK.

5. Click an insertion point after the Airfare form field, press Tab, type *Payment Method:*, press Tab again, and click the Drop-Down Form Field button on the Forms toolbar.

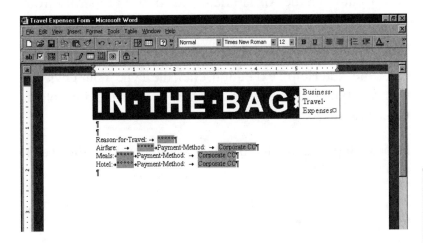

The Drop-Down Form Field button

6. Click the Form Field Options button, type *Corporate CC* in the Drop-Down Item box, and click the Add button. Then type *Personal CC* in the Drop-Down Item box, click the Add button, and click OK. Word inserts the first item in the list as the default—in this case, *Corporate CC.*

7. Click an insertion point after the new field and press Enter to add a blank line. Then move the pointer into the selection bar to the left of the Airfare line and, when the pointer changes to a hollow, right-pointing arrow, click to select the line.

8. Click the Copy button to copy the line, press Ctrl+End to move the insertion point to the blank line at the bottom of the document, and click the Paste button twice.

9. Change the second Airfare to Meals and the third one to Hotel. Your form now looks like the one shown here:

Editing Forms

The travel expenses form is taking shape. To edit the form's labels, you can use ordinary text editing techniques, but if you want to edit the form's fields, you must use the Form Field Options dialog box. Follow the steps on the next page to

Check box form fields

To add a check box field to a form, click the Check Box Form Field button on the Forms toolbar. You can then click the Form Field Options button to change settings such as the size of the check box or the default value (whether it is checked on or off by default).

edit some of the fields to include help text that will appear in the status bar when the fields are selected.

1. Click the Reason for Travel form field once to select it, and then click the Form Field Options button on the Forms toolbar.

Adding help text ───────────▶ 2. In the Text Form Field Options dialog box, click the Add Help Text button to display this dialog box:

3. Click the Type Your Own option and type *Enter the name of the show or conference* in the box below. Then click OK two times. (The help text is not displayed in the status bar until you turn on document protection, which you'll do on page 117.)

4. Now right-click the Airfare field and choose Properties from the shortcut menu to display the Text Form Field Options dialog box again.

5. Click the Add Help Text button, click the Type Your Own option, and type *Enter the total dollar amount* in the box below. Click OK twice.

6. Repeat steps 4 and 5 to add the same help text to the Meals and Hotel fields.

Now let's edit the drop-down list fields by adding some help text. Follow these steps:

1. Double-click the first Payment Method field to automatically open the Drop-Down Form Field Options dialog box.

2. Click the Add Help Text button, click the Type Your Own option, and type *Click the down arrow to display the payment method options.* Click OK twice to enter the changes.

Using AutoText for help

To speed up the entry of often-used help text, you can create AutoText entries (see page 36). You can then click AutoText Entry in the Form Field Help Text dialog box and select the appropriate AutoText name from a list to have the corresponding text appear in the status bar.

3. Repeat steps 1 and 2 to add the same help text to the other two Payment Method fields.

4. When you have finished adding the help text, click the Save button to save your work.

Formatting Forms

Now that you have the fields set up the way you want them, you can format the form to spruce up its appearance, as well as make it easier to read. You want to make some adjustments to the tabs, but before you do that, you should take care of any other character and paragraph formatting. To format the text of a form, you use the same techniques you use in any other Word document. Let's apply some basic formatting now:

1. Select the *Reason for Travel:* label (but not the field that follows it) and click the Bold button. Repeat this step for all of the other labels.

2. Now select the entire form (except the header) and choose Paragraph from the Format menu.

3. In the Spacing section, change the Before and After settings to 3 pt and click OK. Your form now looks like this:

As you can see, the tab settings need to be adjusted so that the fields line up. Follow the steps on the next page to make those adjustments.

1. Select the entire form, click the Tab button until it displays a left-aligned tab (see page 96), and then click the 1½-inch mark on the ruler. Word inserts a left-aligned tab on the ruler and moves the text appropriately.

2. Click the 2¾-inch mark on the ruler to set another tab, and then set a final tab at the 4¼-inch mark.

   Hmmm... The space between the fields is a little too wide. But instead of starting over, let's adjust the tabs on the ruler, as follows:

Adjusting tab settings with the ruler

1. With the form still selected, point to the tab at the 2¾-inch mark on the ruler, hold down the left mouse button, and drag the tab to the left to the 2¼-inch mark. Word adjusts the position of the *Payment Method* label.

2. Now repeat step 1 to move the tab at the 4¼-inch mark to the 3¾-inch mark on the ruler. The form now looks like this:

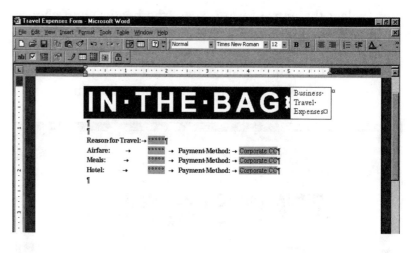

More about using the ruler to set tabs

When you manually set a tab using the ruler (or using the Tabs command), the tab takes effect for the paragraph that contains the insertion point or selected paragraphs only. To remove a custom tab, point to it, hold down the left mouse button, and then drag the tab away from the ruler. Double-clicking a tab on the ruler opens the Tabs dialog box, where you can quickly customize that tab. For example, you can change its Alignment or Leader setting. (See the tip on page 94 for more information about the Tabs dialog box.)

Calculations in Forms

Forms like the travel expenses form often involve calculations. Why perform them manually when you can have Word do them for you? As you saw earlier on page 104, if you enter the values to be calculated in a table, Word can use cell references to perform the calculations. Let's experiment by adding a table of miscellaneous cash expenses that need to be totaled, by following the steps on the facing page.

1. Press Ctrl+End to move to the bottom of the Travel Expenses Form document. Press Enter a couple of times to add some space between the upper portion of the form and the table you are about to add.

2. Type *Miscellaneous (Cash):* and then press Enter.

3. Click the Insert Table button, hold down the mouse button, and drag through two columns and five rows in the table grid.

4. In the first cell, type *Mileage:*, press Tab, and click the Text Form Field button on the Forms toolbar.

5. Click the Form Field Options button and change the Type to Number and the Number Format to the fifth option (the one with the dollar signs). Then click OK.

6. Click an insertion point in the first cell of the second row and type *Parking:*. Press the Down Arrow key and type *Tolls:*. Press the Down Arrow key again and type *Taxis:*.

7. Next copy the form field in the Mileage row and paste it into the second column of the Parking, Tolls, and Taxis rows. Your table now looks like this one:

Now it's time to add the formula that will total the miscellaneous cash expenses. Follow these steps:

1. Click an insertion point in the first cell of the last row. Type *TOTAL:* and press Tab.

Inserting a calculation field

2. Click the Text Form Field button on the Forms toolbar and then click the Form Field Options button.

3. In the Type drop-down list, select Calculation.

4. Click an insertion point in the Expression edit box after the equal sign (=) and type *SUM(B1:B4)*. This expression (formula) tells Word to total the values in the first through fourth cells of the second column (B).

5. In the Number Format drop-down list, select the fifth option and then click OK.

Let's finish up the form with some simple formatting:

1. Select the title above the table and click the Bold button.

2. Next select the first column of the table and make it bold.

3. Move the pointer to the column border between the two columns and drag to the left to about the 1½-inch mark so that the form fields in the table left-align with the form fields in the top section of the form. Then reduce the width of the second column. The form now looks like this one:

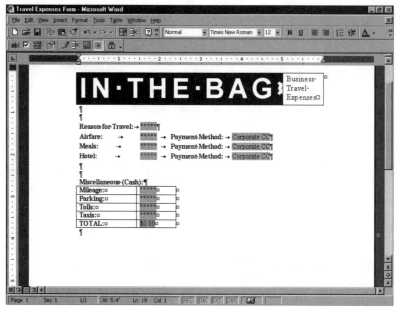

4. Before moving on to the next section, save the form.

Saving Forms as Templates

Once you create a form, you will usually want to save it as a template. You can then access it at any time and fill in the appropriate information, just as you did in Chapter 3 with the memo template (see page 60). But before you can save your form as a template, you must *protect* the document so that only the fields can be changed, not the labels or structure. Protect the Travel Expenses Form document now by following these steps:

1. Click the Protect Form button on the Forms toolbar.

The Protect Form button

2. Try to click an insertion point in the header or labels, or in front of an empty paragraph mark. You can no longer change text in the document unless it appears in a form field.

Now let's save the document as a template so that you can try filling it in:

1. First close the Forms toolbar by right-clicking it and deselecting Forms on the shortcut menu.

2. Next choose Save As from the File menu. In the Save As Type drop-down list, select Document Template. Word changes the Save In location to the C:\Windows\Application Data\Microsoft\Templates folder.

3. Click Save to save the Travel Expenses Form template in the default location.

4. Close the template.

Filling in Forms

You now have a travel expenses form template available for use at any time, but you have yet to see how the form works. Let's open the template now and fill in some information for a trade show in Denver. Follow these steps:

1. Choose New from the File menu, and on the General tab, double-click the Travel Expenses Form icon. Word opens the form with the Reason for Travel form field highlighted.

More about document protection

Word offers several types of document protection via the Protect Document command on the Tools menu. In addition to protecting all but the fields of a form, you can select the Forms option and then click the Sections button to protect sections of the form only. Or, to protect a document from changes by other people but allow them to add comments to the document, select the Comments option. You can allow changes to the document but tell Word to keep track of the editing by selecting the Tracked Changes option. And you can also assign a password of up to 15 characters that must be entered before Word will unprotect the document. (Note that passwords are case-sensitive.)

2. First save the document by choosing Save As from the File menu, typing *Denver Show Expenses* as the filename, and clicking Save.

3. Type *Denver Show* in the Reason for Travel field and press Tab. Word skips over the Airfare label and moves to its field.

4. Type *610* and press Tab. Word automatically formats the number as currency, as you specified earlier when you created the form field.

5. A corporate credit card was used for the plane tickets, so press Tab to leave the entry as is.

6. In the Meals field, type *175.5*. Press Tab, click the down arrow to the right of Corporate CC, and select Personal CC from the drop-down list. Then press Tab.

7. Type *420* in the Hotel field, press Tab twice to leave the payment method as is, and then type the following numbers in the appropriate form fields, pressing Tab to move from one field to the next:

   Mileage: *65*
   Parking: *25*
   Tolls: *0*
   Taxi: *25.5*

8. Press Tab again. Word moves to the top of the document, skipping the TOTAL field, which contains *$0.00*.

Does this mean that Word has not completed the calculation? Not at all. Word simply has not been told to update the contents of the TOTAL field. You could attach a macro to this field to prompt updating, but the topic of macros is beyond the scope of this book (check Word's Help feature if you're interested). You can accomplish the same thing by making a simple adjustment in the Options dialog box and printing the form, so let's take this easier route:

1. Choose Options from the Tools menu and click the Print tab.

Saving form data only

If you want to accumulate the data items entered in multiple copies of a form in a database, you can save only the data by choosing Options from the Tools menu, clicking the Save tab, and selecting the Save Data Only For Forms check box. Then choose Save Copy As from the File menu to have Word create a text-only file with each data item enclosed in quotation marks and separated from adjacent items by commas. This file is then ready to be imported into a database.

2. In the Printing Options section, click the Update Fields check box to turn it on, and then click OK.

3. Click the Print button to print the form. After you have printed the form, the number in the calculated field is displayed on your screen. Look at page 93 for a sample of what the printed form looks like.

4. Save and close Denver Show Expenses.

Customizing Form Templates

You've now seen how to create and fill in a Word form, but what if you want to create another form that is similar to an existing one? Simple. As a demonstration, let's quickly customize the business travel expenses form to create a form that tracks marketing project expenses:

1. Choose New from the File menu, and on the General tab, double-click Travel Expenses Form.

Saving a template with a new name

2. Choose Save As from the File menu and change the Save As Type setting to Document Template. Word changes the Save In setting to the Templates subfolder.

3. Type *Marketing Project Expenses Form* as the new template's filename and click Save.

Now let's customize the form:

1. Display the Forms toolbar by right-clicking a toolbar and choosing Forms from the shortcut menu.

2. Click the Protect Form button to turn off form protection so that you are able to customize the header and labels for the new form.

Turning off form protection

3. Select the words *Business Travel* in the form header and replace them with *Marketing Project*. (Adjust the column width if necessary.)

4. Next change *Reason for Travel* to *Project* and then continue changing the labels as shown on the next page.

Airfare	*Radio*
Meals	*Printing*
Hotel	*Magazine*
Miscellaneous (Cash)	*Miscellaneous Expenses*
Mileage	*Freight*
Parking	*Office Supplies*
Tolls	*Design Costs*

5. Change all *Payment Method* labels to *Payment Terms*.

6. Select the Taxis row in the table and choose Delete and then Rows from the Table menu. The form now looks like this:

Now let's adjust some of the form fields:

Editing a calculation field

1. Because you have deleted a row in the table, double-click the TOTAL form field, change the cell reference in the Expression edit box from B1:B4 to B1:B3, and click OK.

Editing a drop-down field

2. Double-click the first Payment Terms form field, and with Corporate CC selected in the Items list, click Remove. Click Remove again to delete Personal CC from the list.

3. In the Drop-Down Item edit box, type *Net 30*, click Add, type *Net 60*, click Add, type *Net 90*, click Add, and then click OK.

4. Select the second Payment Terms form field and delete it. Then copy and paste the first Payment Terms form field to the second Payment Terms field.

5. Repeat step 4 to update the last Payment Terms form field.

6. Finally, double-click the Project form field, click the Add Help Text button, change *show or conference* to *project*, and then click OK twice.

7. Click the Protect Form button and close the Forms toolbar. Your form now looks something like the one shown below.

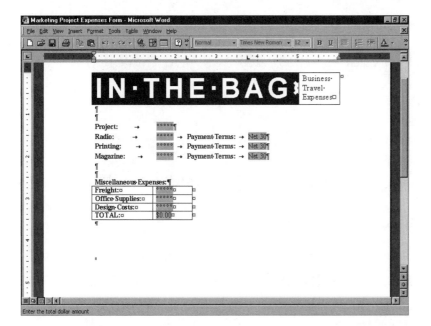

8. Save and close the template.

9. If you want, open a new document based on the Marketing Project Expenses Form template and try filling in the form.

   As you have seen, tables and forms give you two ways to organize information in Word. In the next chapter, you'll look at ways you can use information created in other programs in your Word documents.

5

More Visual Effects

You use WordArt to create fancy text as you develop a letterhead template and a masthead template. Then you import and manipulate a graphic. You create a graph with Microsoft Graph and import a spreadsheet from Microsoft Excel as a table.

The masthead you create here is for a press release, but you can also use mastheads for newsletters, invitations, and announcements.

Documents created and concepts covered:

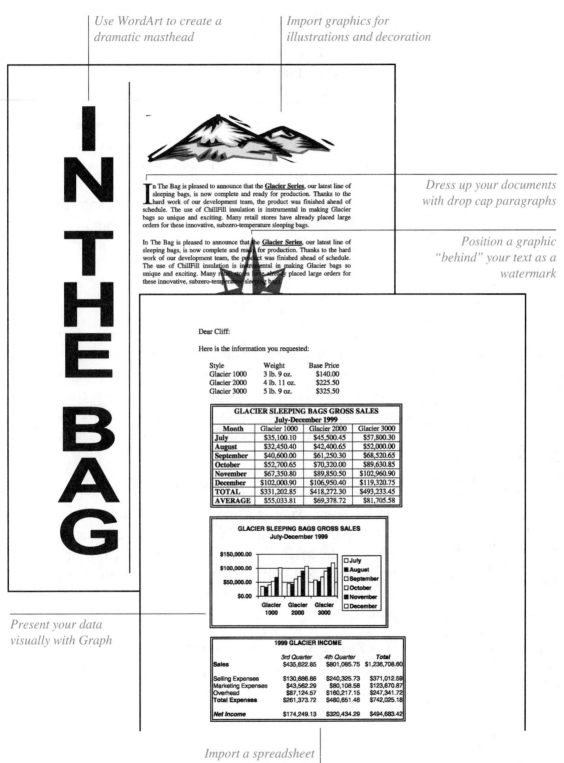

While following the examples in the preceding chapters, you've learned a lot about Word's formatting capabilities and how to combine formats to create professional-looking documents. However, there may be times when the needs of a particular document exceed Word's capabilities. That's when you will want to enlist the help of other programs.

In this chapter, we start by showing you how to create special effects with text and how you can incorporate graphics into Word documents. Then you learn how to create graphs to visually present facts and figures. And for those times when you've already set up your information in a spreadsheet or database program and don't relish the thought of having to recreate it in Word, we'll show you how to import a spreadsheet or database as a Word table.

Text as Graphics

You have seen in earlier chapters some ways to format text to make it more visually appealing. But sometimes, this type of text formatting won't be quite spectacular enough. In this section, you'll look at a couple of techniques for giving documents more pizazz. You can then experiment on your own with different ways of combining effects to create the look you want.

Creating Special Effects with WordArt

Do you want to create a text wave across the page or rotate a title in order to grab people's attention? Well, that's the specialty of the Insert WordArt button on the Drawing toolbar. By embedding a WordArt object in a document, you can produce an eye-catching look that can be handled by almost any printer.

Creating a Letterhead Template

For our first example, let's experiment with WordArt by quickly creating a letterhead for In The Bag. Follow the steps on the facing page.

Working with objects

An object is any element within the document that can be manipulated independently of the document's text. It can be a block of text, a graphic, a table, a graph, and so on. You can incorporate objects from external sources into your documents in three ways: (1) You can copy and paste an object into a document, in which case the copy becomes an integral part of the document and is stored with it. (2) You can embed the object in the document, in which case it is stored with the document but retains information about the program that created it. If you want to change the object, double-click it to open it in the source program, edit the object, and close the program to return to the document with the changes in place. (3) You can link the object to the document, in which case the object exists in a separate file but is displayed in the document. Any changes you make to the object's file will be reflected in the version displayed in the document. (See the tip on page 146 for more information about embedding and linking.)

1. With a new, blank document on your screen, click the Drawing button on the Standard toolbar to display the Drawing toolbar along the bottom of your screen. (If you are not in print layout view, Word switches to it now.)

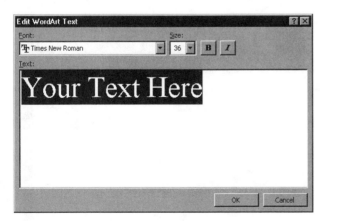

The Drawing button

2. Press Enter and then press the Up Arrow key to move back to the top of the page.

3. Next click the Insert WordArt button on the Drawing toolbar to display this WordArt Gallery dialog box:

The Insert WordArt button

4. Click the second option in the fourth row and click OK to display this dialog box:

5. Type *IN THE BAG*, change the font to Arial, and click OK.

6. Close the WordArt toolbar. Your screen now looks as shown on the next page.

The WordArt toolbar

The WordArt toolbar comes with a variety of buttons. To edit the WordArt text or change its font and font size, click the Edit Text button. To change the style, click the WordArt Gallery button to re-display its dialog box. To change the color, size, or position, or the way regular text wraps around the WordArt object, simply click the Format WordArt button. The remaining buttons allow you to alter the shape, rotation, text wrapping, letter height, orientation, alignment, and character spacing of the WordArt object. You can also change the shape of the object by dragging the yellow diamond handle up or down. As you drag it, the dotted outline shows the approximate shape the object will assume when you re-lease the mouse button.

The WordArt object is "floating" at the top of the document. Let's resize it to make its shape more triangular:

Sizing a WordArt object

1. With the object selected (surrounded by white squares called *handles*), point to the right middle handle. When the pointer becomes a two-headed arrow, drag inward about ½ inch.

2. Next drag the bottom middle handle downward about ½ inch. The WordArt object now looks something like this:

Not bad for a start. To finish off the letterhead, let's center the WordArt object at the top of the page and add an address below the company name:

1. Point to the WordArt text and when the pointer changes to a four-headed arrow, drag the object so that its base sits at about the 1¼-inch mark on the vertical ruler and its peak sits at approximately the 3-inch mark on the horizontal ruler.

2. Press Ctrl+End and press Enter until the insertion point is about ¼ inch below the WordArt object. Then click the Center button on the Formatting toolbar.

3. Type *1200 Yukon Avenue, Anchorage, AK 99502*. Then press Enter again to add a blank line.

4. Select the address text, change the font size to 11, and then make it bold.

5. Fine-tune the placement of the WordArt object so that it is centered above the address. Here are the results:

← Repositioning a WordArt object

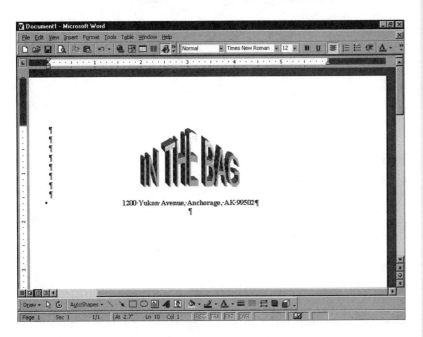

Because In The Bag is likely to use this letterhead often, it makes sense to save the letterhead document as a template. Follow the steps on the next page.

Floating objects

By default, Word inserts WordArt text as a "floating" object on a separate drawing layer so that you can position it exactly where you want it. Also by default, the object is anchored to the paragraph that contained the insertion point when you created the object, and it will move with that paragraph. To control how an object interacts with the text of your document, click the Format WordArt button on the WordArt toolbar, click the Layout tab of the Format WordArt dialog box, and specify a wrapping style. You can specify that the text should wrap around, through, or above and below an object. If you click the Advanced button, Word displays the Advanced Layout dialog box. On the Picture Position tab, you can deselect the Move Object With Text check box to break the object's link with its paragraph mark.

1. Choose Save As from the File menu.

2. In the Save As dialog box, select Document Template from the Save As Type drop-down list, type *Letterhead* in the File Name box, and click the Save button. Then close the new template.

Creating a Masthead Template

Now let's move on to something a little more complex. This time, you will use WordArt and the Drawing toolbar to design a masthead template for In The Bag. You'll put the company's masthead down the left side of the document and leave space for text, such as a press release, to the right. Follow these steps to try this out:

1. Click the New button on the Standard toolbar to open a new document.

2. In order to put the masthead to the left and the text to the right, you need to set up columns in your document. Click the Columns button and drag through two columns.

3. Choose Break from the Insert menu, select Column Break, and then click OK to move the insertion point to the top of the second column.

4. Click the Insert WordArt button on the Drawing toolbar, select the last option in the top row, and click OK.

5. Type *IN THE BAG*, change the font to Arial, change the size to 80, and make the text bold. Then click OK to return to your document.

6. Close the WordArt toolbar.

Now let's move the WordArt object to the desired location in the document:

1. Move the pointer over the WordArt object. When the pointer changes to a four-headed arrow, drag the object to the left side of the screen and then downward about ¾ inch from the top, as shown on the facing page.

Adding page borders

For some documents, it might be appropriate to add a border around each page. To add a page border, first choose Borders And Shading from the Format menu and then click the Page Border tab. You can select from many border art styles in the Art drop-down list to apply a fancy border instead of a line border. (You may be prompted to install this feature.) If you want the border to appear only on a particular side of the page, click Custom in the Setting section. Then, in the Preview section, click where you want the border to appear. To make one appear only on a particular page or section of the document, click the appropriate option in the Apply To drop-down list. If you need to specify the exact location of a page border, you can click the Options button and then make your specifications. To remove a page border, redisplay the Page Border tab of the Borders And Shading dialog box and click None in the Setting section.

2. Scroll the bottom of the page into view and then drag the bottom middle handle of the WordArt object downward. Release the mouse button when you have about a 1-inch bottom margin.

3. Click the Print Preview button to see these results:

4. Click the Close button to return to print layout view, make any other necessary adjustments, and then save the document as a template called *Masthead*. (Save often from now on.)

Let's add a side border to the object to visually separate the masthead from the text of the press release, which you will add later. Follow the steps on the next page.

Inserting special symbols

Sometimes you may want to use special symbols in a document, such as a pointing hand to draw the reader's attention. To insert a special symbol, position the insertion point, choose Symbol from the Insert menu, and select the font (Wingdings is a good one if you're looking for cute little pictures). Then click the symbol you want, click Insert, and click Close. If you use a symbol often, you can create a keyboard shortcut for the symbol by clicking the Shortcut Key button in the Symbol dialog box and specifying a shortcut that starts with the Ctrl or Alt key or a combination of the two.

The Line button

1. Deselect the WordArt object by clicking anywhere in the document. Then click the Line button on the Drawing toolbar.

2. Point about ¼ inch to the right and ½ inch below the bottom of the WordArt text, hold down the left mouse button, and drag upward to about ½ inch above the WordArt text. (If the line is crooked, simply move the mouse to the left or right until the line straightens up.) Then release the mouse button.

The Line Style button

3. With the line selected, click the Line Style button on the Drawing toolbar and select the 1½-pt line style from the list of options. The masthead template now looks like the one shown here in print preview:

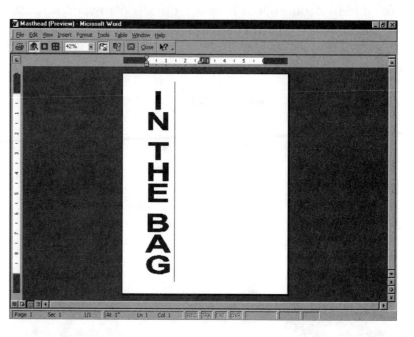

4. If you need to lengthen or shorten the line, point to its top or bottom handle and drag in the appropriate direction.

Now let's add some placeholder press-release text to the template. (You can replace the text when you create a press release based on this template.) Follow these steps:

1. First adjust the size of the masthead column. Point to the column marker on the ruler, and when the pointer changes to a double-headed arrow, drag the marker to the left until the dotted vertical line aligns with the side border you just drew.

Editing WordArt objects

If you want to make changes to a WordArt object after you have inserted it into a document, double-click the object to display the Edit WordArt Text dialog box as well as the WordArt toolbar. You can then edit the text or use the dialog box's buttons to make adjustments. When you're finished, click OK to return to your document. While the WordArt object is selected, you can make adjustments using the WordArt toolbar's buttons (see the tip on page 125).

2. Click an insertion point in the second column.

Copying text using a scrap

3. Open Glacier Memo (the document you created in Chapter 3), click its Restore button (the middle button at the right end of the title bar), and size the window to take up half the screen.

4. Resize the Masthead window so that part of the Windows desktop is visible.

5. Activate the Glacier Memo window, select the first main paragraph, and drag it onto the desktop. When a plus sign appears below the pointer, release the mouse button. Word creates a document "scrap" icon on the desktop, representing your copied text, as shown here:

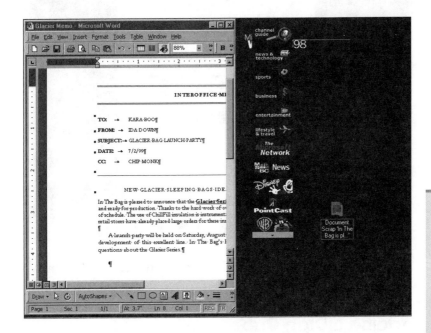

6. Close Glacier Memo and then drag a copy of the document scrap icon from the desktop to the left of the paragraph mark in the second column of the masthead template. Word inserts the text in the document.

Bookmarks

If you frequently use a specific piece of text in a document, you might want to set a bookmark in the document so that you can quickly jump to that text. Click an insertion point at the beginning of the text and choose Bookmark from the Insert menu. In the Bookmark dialog box, enter a name for the bookmark and click Add. When you need to jump to the text, choose Go To from the Edit menu, select Bookmark in the Go To What list, select the name of the bookmark from the Enter Bookmark Name drop-down list, click Go To, and then click Close.

7. Maximize the Masthead window. Then select the newly inserted paragraph and the paragraph mark that follows it, and click the Copy button.

8. Press Enter to insert an extra paragraph mark after the text paragraph and then click the Paste button.

9. Click the paste button twice more so that you have a total of four paragraphs, as shown here (we've reduced the magnification to 50% to show all the paragraphs):

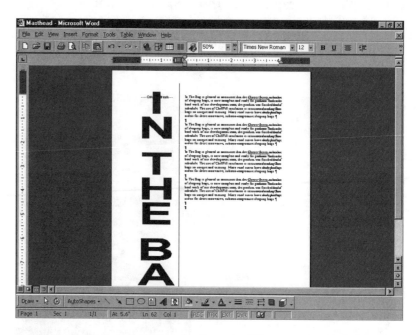

10. Save the template but don't close it. Then turn off the Drawing toolbar.

Adding a Drop Cap

A simple way to add a designer touch to a document is to use Word's built-in drop cap (for *dropped capital letter*) format. Drop caps are used in the first paragraph of each chapter in this book. Drop caps can also enhance newsletters, reports, and other documents that receive public scrutiny. Insert a drop cap in the first paragraph of the press release text by following the steps on the facing page.

1. Click an insertion point to the left of the first paragraph and press Enter to add some space above it.

2. Choose Drop Cap from the Format menu to display this dialog box:

If you select Dropped, Word makes the first letter of the active paragraph the height of three lines of text. You can adjust the drop cap's font, height, and distance from the following text in the above dialog box.

3. Select the Dropped option and click OK. Then click anywhere in the first paragraph, which now looks like this:

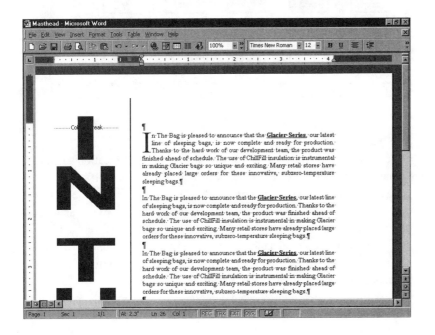

Importing Graphics

Ready-made graphics

Word 2000 comes with a collection of ready-made graphics files suitable for many different types of documents. As a demonstration, you'll place one of these graphics at both the top and bottom of the press release. Follow these steps:

1. Click an insertion point to the left of the blank paragraph mark at the top of the press release text, press Enter once to add a bit more space, and then press the Up Arrow key once.

Inserting a graphic

2. Choose Picture and then Clip Art from the Insert menu to display a Clip Gallery window like the one shown here:

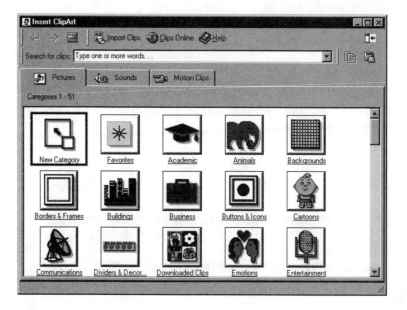

Inline graphics

Unlike WordArt objects, graphics are inline by default (see the tip on page 127). This means that they are not on a separate drawing layer but are inserted directly in the document at the insertion point. To convert an inline to a floating graphic, select the graphic, display the Format Picture dialog box, and on the Layout tab, select a wrapping style other than In Line With Text.

Using PhotoDraw

Microsoft PhotoDraw 2000 is a powerful new graphics creation and manipulation program that is available with some editions of Office 2000 or as a stand-alone application. You can draw new graphics from scratch or using templates and shapes that come with the program. Or you can modify existing graphics with special effects that you apply in layers until the original is barely recognizable. You can even surround graphics with outlines of various shapes. PhotoDraw comes with a huge supply of graphics to choose from, or you can use its capabilities to "doctor" your own graphics. With all the permutations and combinations available, the possibilities are virtually unlimited.

3. Scroll through the categories and click Nature.

4. Scroll the previews, select the mountains with a flag, and click the Insert Clip button that appears.

The Insert Clip button

5. Close the window to view the graphic at the top of the template, as shown here:

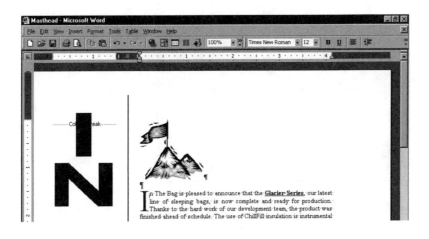

Sizing and Positioning Graphics

After you import a graphic, you can change its size and shape to suit the needs of your document. For example, you might want to turn the graphic into a small logo, or you might want to enlarge it so that it occupies most of the page. Let's experiment a bit:

1. Click the graphic once to select it. When the Picture toolbar appears, double-click its title bar to dock it at the bottom of the screen.

2. To increase the graphic's size, point to the handle in the bottom right corner, and when the pointer changes to a two-headed arrow, drag it downward and to the right.

If you drag the corner handles, you change the size of the graphic without changing the ratio of its width to its height. If you drag the handles in the middle of the sides of the frame, you do change this ratio. You can control the width-to-height ratio more precisely by changing settings in a dialog box instead of dragging. Follow the steps on the next page.

Drawing your own graphics

You can create your own simple drawings in Word. Click the Drawing button on the Standard toolbar to show the Drawing toolbar across the bottom of your screen. Then use the Line, Arrow, Rectangle, and Oval buttons to draw the corresponding shapes. You can also click the Auto-Shapes button to display a pop-up menu of options that allow you to create more complex shapes, such as stars. Use the remaining buttons to manipulate your drawing in a variety of ways; for example, you can change its color and orientation.

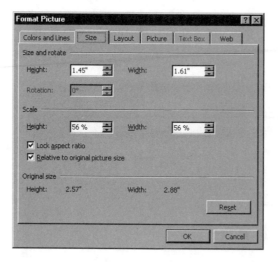

1. With the graphic selected, click the Format Picture button on the Picture toolbar. When Word displays the Format Picture dialog box, click the Size tab to see these options:

2. In the Scale section, deselect Lock Aspect Ratio. Then set the Height option to 60% and the Width option to 30%, and click OK. Here's the result:

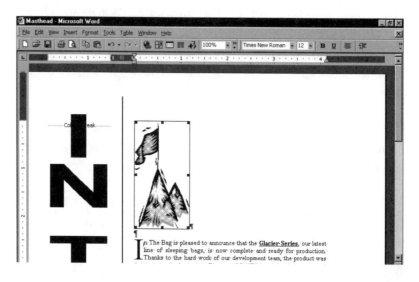

If you want to use part of the graphic, you can change the size of the frame that contains it without changing the size of the graphic. This adjustment has the effect of "cropping" the parts of the graphic that you don't want shown. Here are the steps:

1. With the graphic selected, click the Format Picture button on the Picture toolbar.

2. On the Picture tab of the Format Picture dialog box, change the Top setting in the Crop From section to *1.5"* and click OK. When the dialog box closes, this is what you see:

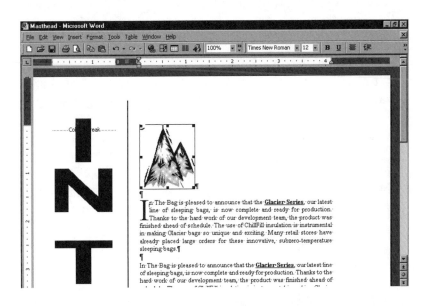

You can also use the Crop button on the Picture toolbar to crop graphics. Select the graphic, click the Crop button, use the cropping tool to drag the appropriate handle to change the size of the graphic's frame, and then click the Crop button again to turn off the cropping tool.

The Crop button

3. Click the Reset Picture button on the Picture toolbar to restore the graphic to its original unscaled, uncropped size and proportions.

The Reset Picture button

Let's be more precise about the graphic's size and location:

1. Click the Format Picture button on the Picture toolbar and on the Size tab, set the Height to *1"* and the Width to *4"*.

2. Click the Layout tab and change the Wrapping setting to Square. (To enter an absolute position for the graphic on the page, you must select a wrapping style other than In Line With Text to turn the graphic into a floating object.) Next click the Advanced button to display the Advanced Layout dialog box. On the Picture Position tab, enter *1.7"* and Margin as the Horizontal Absolute Position, and then enter *0"* and Margin as the Vertical Absolute Position. Click OK.

Editing graphics

To change a graphic you have created or one you have added using the Picture command, click the graphic to display the Picture toolbar. You can then use the buttons on the Picture toolbar to achieve the desired effect. When you are finished, click anywhere outside the graphic.

3. On the Picture tab, enter *0.3"* as the Left setting and *1.6"* as the Top setting. Then click OK to return to the document.

4. If necessary, adjust the settings manually to size and position the graphic exactly where you want it.

Copying Graphics

For fun, let's put the same graphic at the bottom of the press release text with this simple copy-and-paste procedure:

1. With the graphic selected, click the Copy button and then click the Paste button.

2. Click the Zoom box, type *40*, and press Enter to change the magnification to 40%.

3. Drag the copy of the graphic below the press release text. Here are the results:

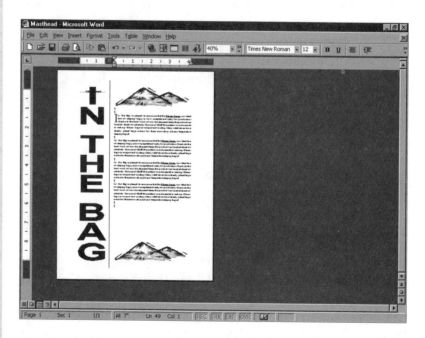

Using Graphics as Watermarks

Let's add another graphic to the template to serve as a *watermark*. A watermark is a logo, picture, or text that appears "behind" a document. (Diplomas and stock certificates often sport watermarks.) For this example, you'll insert a watermark in the template's header so that it will appear on every page of the document. Try this:

Using text boxes

For more flexibility with text, you can insert a text box in a document and then type the text directly in the box. Word treats text boxes as objects that can be positioned and sized on the page just like any other object. To add a text box, either choose Text Box from the Insert menu or click the Text Box button on the Drawing toolbar. Then drag a box on the document using the crosshair pointer. When you release the mouse button, Word displays a box containing the insertion point, waiting for you to type your text. You can format and edit the text in the usual way. You can also use buttons on the Drawing toolbar to format the text box, or choose Text Box from the Format menu to adjust its size, position, and text-wrapping settings. You can use buttons on the Text Box toolbar to change the direction of the text, link text boxes, and move among linked boxes.

1. Return the document magnification to 100% and then choose Header And Footer from the View menu.

2. Click the Show/Hide Document Text button on the Header And Footer toolbar. Word hides all of the text and graphics in the press release.

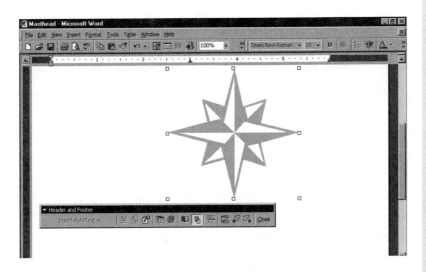

The Show/Hide Document Text button

3. Choose Picture and then Clip Art from the Insert menu to display the Clip Gallery window shown earlier on page 134.

4. Display the Navigation category, select the compass symbol, click the Insert Clip button, and close the window.

5. Double-click the graphic to open the Format Picture dialog box.

6. On the Picture tab, click the arrow to the right of the Color edit box in the Image Control section and select Watermark. Then change the Contrast setting in the Image control section to 50%.

7. Display the Layout tab and click Behind Text. Then click the Advanced button, enter *2.5"* and Margin as the Horizontal Absolute Position setting, and enter *2.5"* and Margin as the Vertical Absolute Position setting. Click OK.

8. On the Size tab, change the Height setting in the Scale section to 500%. Click the Width setting, which adjusts to 500%. Click OK. Your screen looks something like this:

Adding a watermark to one page only

In our example, you add a watermark to the header so that the watermark appears on all the pages of the document. If you want to add a watermark to just one page, insert the graphic, click the Image Control button on the Picture toolbar, and select Watermark. Then click the Text Wrapping button and select Behind Text. Word converts the watermark to a floating graphic so that you can manually move and resize it, or you can change the settings in the Advanced Layout dialog box to make more precise adjustments.

9. Click Close on the Header And Footer toolbar to return to the template and then click the Print Preview button to view the results, shown here:

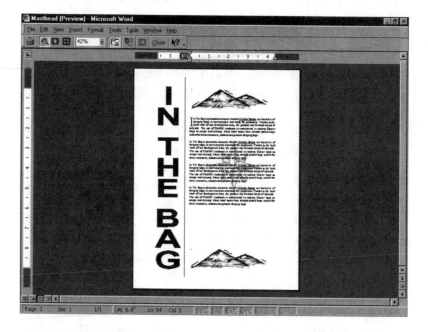

If you need to make any further adjustments to the watermark, return to header and footer view, click the Show/Hide Document Text button, and click the watermark graphic to select it. Then either manually move or resize it, or click the Format Picture button and make your changes in the dialog box.

10. When you finish, save and close the masthead template.

We've thrown a lot of graphics into this example. For your own documents, you'll want to limit the use of graphics to avoid a cluttered look that makes your message hard to read.

Using Graph

With Word, you can cut or copy charts and graphs from other applications and then paste them into a Word document. But Word also comes with Microsoft Graph, a program you can use to create graph objects based on information in a Word document. Let's experiment using part of the table you constructed in the memo in Chapter 4. Follow these steps:

1. Open the Sales Memo document and save it as *Sales Memo 2*.

Turning off graphics display

Inserting graphics in a document can slow down the rate at which you can scroll through the text. With inline graphics, you can increase the scrolling speed. Choose Options from the Tools menu, click the View tab, click Picture Placeholders in the Show section, and click OK. Word substitutes placeholders (empty frames) for the graphics. Reverse this procedure to redisplay the graphics.

2. With the Zoom setting at 100%, click an insertion point below the table and press Enter twice to add some space.

3. Select rows two through eight of the table—everything but the title, total, and average rows—and click the Copy button.

4. Choose Object from the Insert menu to display this dialog box: ←

Inserting an object

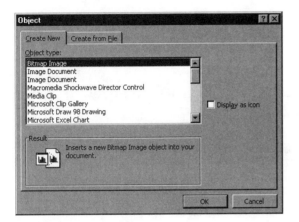

5. Scroll the list of object types, which reflects the programs installed on your computer.

6. Select Microsoft Graph 2000 Chart and click OK. Word starts Graph, which enters the copied table data in a datasheet and plots it in a default format, as shown below. (Graph's menu bar and Standard and Formatting toolbars have replaced Word's at the top of the window.)

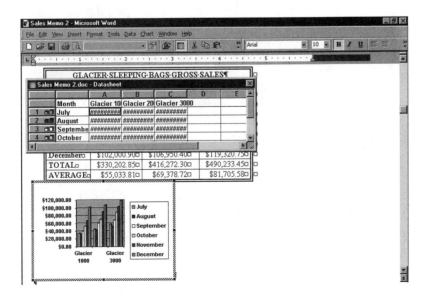

7. Click the datasheet's Close button.

The graph is a little crowded, so let's simplify it by switching from a three-dimensional to a two-dimensional format. (You can work with the graph only when it is selected. If you accidentally click outside the graph, double-click it to reselect it and reactivate the Graph program.) Follow these steps:

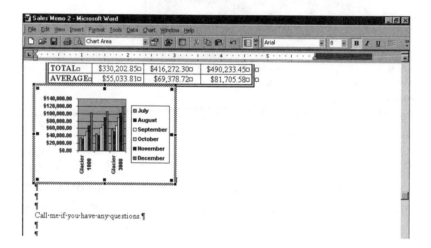

The Chart Type button

1. To change the format, click the arrow to the right of the Chart Type button on Graph's Standard toolbar to display a palette of options.

2. Click the first column chart option in the third row to change from 3-D to 2-D, as shown here:

Not a bad beginning, but the graph obviously needs some adjustments. So that all the labels on the category (x) axis are displayed, let's make the graph object's window a little larger. Try this:

1. Point to the bottom right corner of the graph. When the pointer changes to a double-headed arrow, drag the border down and to the right until the graph measures about 4 inches by 2½ inches and all the labels are displayed.

2. Now let's add a title and subtitle. First choose Chart Options from the Chart menu and if necessary, click the Titles tab to display the options shown at the top of the facing page.

Importing graphs

To import an existing Microsoft Excel graph into a Word document, the graph must be saved in its own file. Choose Object from the Insert menu and click the Create From File tab. Then click the Browse button, navigate to the graph file you want to open, and click OK. Word inserts a copy of the file in your document. To edit the graph, you must double-click it to activate the Graph program.

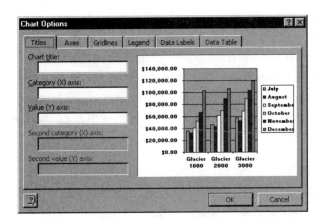

3. Click an insertion point in the Chart Title edit box, type *GLACIER SLEEPING BAGS GROSS SALES*, and click OK.

4. Next select the title text and change the font size to 10 so that the title fits on one line.

5. Click an insertion point at the end of the title, press Enter, and type *July-December 1999*. The graph now looks like the one shown here:

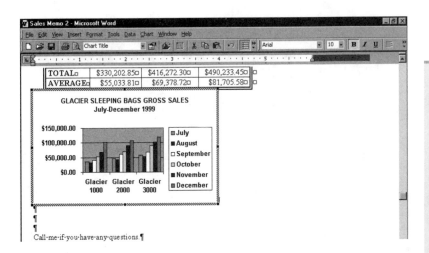

More about the Chart Options command

In addition to adding a title to a graph, you can also add or alter many other graph elements using the Chart Options command. On the Axes tab, you can turn off the display of one or both axes. On the Gridlines tab, you can change the display of gridlines. Click the Legend tab to turn off the legend or change its placement. On the Data Labels tab, you can display data labels for each data point in the graph. And, on the Data Table tab, you can click the Show Data Table check box to display the graph's underlying data as a table below the graph.

6. Click outside the graph frame to close Microsoft Graph and update the graph in Sales Memo 2.

When you return to the document in Word, you can see that the graph has been inserted below the table but not exactly where you want it. Follow the steps on the next page to make a few more adjustments.

Moving a graph

1. If necessary, scroll the window until you see the blank paragraph marks below the graph. Then click the graph once to select it, hold down the left mouse button, and drag the shadow insertion point in front of the first paragraph mark below the graph. When you release the mouse button, the graph moves down to its new position, and a paragraph mark now separates it from the table.

Aligning a graph

2. To align the graph with the table above, make sure the graph is still selected and then drag the top triangle at the left end of the horizontal ruler to the ¼-inch mark.

The graph's frame currently has no border. Let's quickly add a border now:

Adding a border to a graph

1. With the graph selected, choose Borders And Shading from the Format menu.

2. Click Box in the Setting section, select the double-line Style option, select *1½ pt* from the Width drop-down list, and click OK. Here are the results:

Adding borders to objects

To add a border to any graphic object, you select the object and then choose Borders And Shading from the Format menu. Depending on the object type, Word either displays the Border tab of the Borders And Shading dialog box (as it does in the adjacent example), where you can make your selections as usual, or it displays the Colors And Lines tab of the Format Picture dialog box. Here you can change the Color setting to the desired color in the Line section, select a style and weight for the border, and then click OK.

3. Click the Save button to safeguard your work.

To edit the graph, you can simply double-click it to open it in
Microsoft Graph, where you can change data values in the
datasheet, reformat the graph, and change its type.

Editing a graph

Although Graph doesn't offer all the capabilities of dedicated
graphing programs, it is often all you need to quickly generate
visual representations of your data. You might want to spend
a little more time experimenting with this program, using the
simple table you created in Chapter 4 or more complex sets of
your own data.

Importing Spreadsheets

As you've seen, Word allows you to create impressive tables
and perform simple calculations with ease. However, it can't
handle complex formulas and functions the way a spreadsheet program can. On the other hand, though a spreadsheet
program is great for performing calculations, it lacks the
word processing capabilities needed to put together dynamic
reports. Suppose you have gone to a lot of trouble to create a
spreadsheet and you want to include the spreadsheet's data in
a document. It would be frustrating to have to rekey all that
information into a Word table for presentation. Fortunately,
you don't have to. With Word 2000, you can combine the best
of both worlds—the numeric know-how of a spreadsheet program with the word processing proficiency of Word.

To demonstrate, let's import a spreadsheet into the Sales Memo
2 document. (We'll import the one shown below, which we
created with Microsoft Excel 2000.)

	A	B	C	D
1		1999 GLACIER INCOME		
2				
3		3rd Quarter	4th Quarter	Total
4	Sales	$435,622.85	$801,085.75	$1,236,708.60
5				
6	Selling Expenses	$130,686.86	$240,325.73	$371,012.59
7	Marketing Expenses	$43,562.29	$80,108.58	$123,670.87
8	Overhead	$87,124.57	$160,217.15	$247,341.72
9	Total Expenses	$261,373.72	$480,651.46	$742,025.18
10				
11	Net Income	$174,249.13	$320,434.29	$494,683.42
12				
13				
14				

The Insert Microsoft Excel
Worksheet button

To import an Excel file, you can click the Insert Microsoft Excel Worksheet button on the Standard toolbar. But because you might want to import a spreadsheet that was created in another program, we'll show you the most generic method. Follow these steps with your own spreadsheet file (or you can quickly create a version of ours):

1. Click an insertion point to the left of the second blank paragraph mark below the graph in Sales Memo 2. (If necessary, press Enter to add some space.)

2. Choose File from the Insert menu. Word displays the Insert File dialog box.

Linking data from other applications

You can create a dynamic link between spreadsheet or database information and a Word document either by embedding the information as an object in the Word document or by linking the information to the Word document. To utilize the embedding technique, choose Object from the Insert menu, and on the Create From File tab, first select the file, click Link To File, and then click OK. To utilize the linking technique, open the information in the source application and copy it to the Clipboard. Then switch to the Word document, choose Paste Special from the Edit menu, click Paste Link, specify the type of link in the As list, and then click OK. If the linked information changes in its source document, Word will automatically update the Word document when you open it. If the document is already open, you can update the information in the document by choosing the Links command from the Edit menu.

3. In the Files Of Type drop-down list, select All Files. Move to the folder in which the spreadsheet file you want to import is stored and double-click its filename. Word displays the dialog box shown here (you may be prompted to install this feature first):

4. Either accept the default Entire Workbook option or click the arrow to the right of the Open Document edit box and select a worksheet from the drop-down list. If you select a worksheet, you can specify the range you want to import in the Name Or Cell Range edit box. (For example, we selected Sheet1 and specified A1:D11 as the range.) Click OK to start the conversion process. When Word finishes the conversion, the spreadsheet file is inserted as a table at the insertion point.

5. Format the spreadsheet using the table-formatting techniques described on page 102. Here's how our table looks at 50% after we added a border, indented the table, adjusted its size, and made one or two other adjustments:

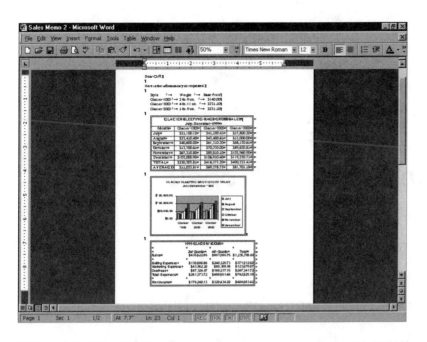

Using only Word's features, you can create some pretty fancy documents. Adding special text effects, a few graphics, and graphs gives those documents real distinction! So be adventurous, and let Word help you generate documents that will make your clients and colleagues sit up and take notice.

Mail Merge:
Form Letters and Labels

It's easy to prepare documents for mail merging with Word. In this chapter, you create a small client database and use it to print form letters. Next you create more complex form letters by inserting conditional statements. Finally, you print a set of mailing labels.

You can use the skills you learn here to make it easier to communicate with any group of people, such as your clients, employees, or club members.

Documents created and concepts covered:

IN THE BAG

1200 Yukon Avenue, Anchorage, AK 99502

Tim Buhr
947 St. Clair Road
Conway, NH 03818

Dear Tim:

Thank you for your recent order of Glacier sleeping bags. Your order of $250 worth of merchandise is greatly appreciated.

We are excited about this new lin[e]
for us to continually improve upo[n]
your comments. Please take a mo[ment]
to us.

We appreciate your input and loo[k]

Sincerely,

Al Pine, President

Print mailing labels using the same set of records

Tim Buhr
947 St. Clair Road
Conway, NH 03818

IN THE BAG

1200 Yukon Avenue, Anchorage, AK 99502

Brooke Trout
The Great Outdoors Inc.
1432 West Colorado Hwy.
Colorado Springs, CO 80901

Dear Brooke:

Thank you for your recent order of Glacier sleeping bags. Your order of $1250 worth of merchandise is greatly appreciated. Because of the size of your order, we are offering you an additional 10% off on your next purchase.

We are excited about this new line and are eager to hear your comments. The best way for us to continually improve upon the standards for our sleeping bags is by addressing your comments. Please take a moment to fill out the enclosed questionnaire and return it to us.

We appreciate your input and look forward to doing business with you again.

Sincerely,

Al Pine, President

Create form letters using name and address records in a data source

Print text for records that meet certain conditions

Most people in the United States have received at least a few personalized form letters. Even kids get them! You know the sort of thing—your name is sprinkled liberally throughout, with a few references to the city in which you live or some other item of personal information. Mail of this sort is an example of the use, and often the abuse, of the mail merge feature available with many word processing programs. We certainly don't want to assist in the destruction of the forests of the world by showing you how to send junk mail to millions of people. But if you'll use your new knowledge wisely and with restraint, we'll introduce you to the mysteries of mail merge.

Actually, with Word 2000, mail merge isn't even all that mysterious. If you have used this feature in other word processors or in other versions of Word, you'll be pleasantly surprised at the ease with which you can create mail merge documents using Word 2000. For those of you who have never used mail merge (or *print merge*, as it is often called), we'll start with a definition.

What Is Mail Merge?

Mail merge is the printing of a bunch of similar documents by merging the information in one document, called the *main document*, with what is essentially a database of variable information in a second document, called the *data source*.

The main document ➝ The main document contains the information that does not change from printout to printout—the text of a form letter, for example—along with placeholders called *merge fields* for the

Merge fields ➝ information that does change and codes that control the merging process. A main document with a typical set of merge fields is shown at the top of the facing page.

The data source ➝ Each word enclosed in chevrons is a name that matches the name of a field in the corresponding data source, also shown on the facing page. As you can see, the data source contains the information that changes with each printout: first name, last name, company, address, and so on. The data in this particular data source is stored in a Word table, but you can use

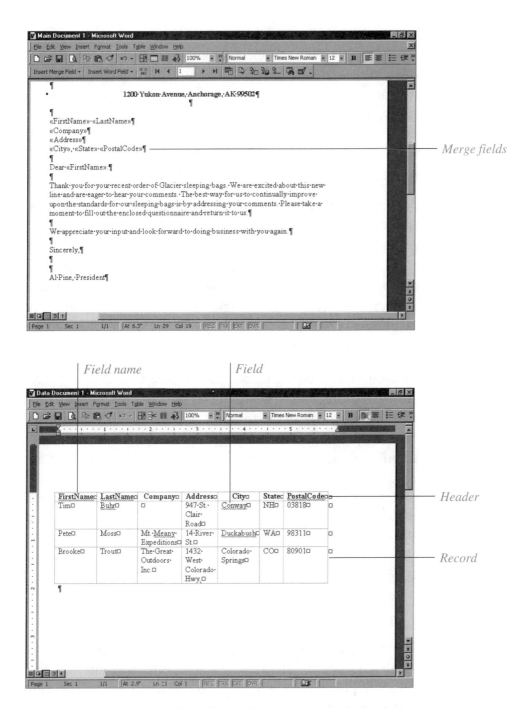

Merge fields

Field name

Field

Header

Record

other formats, such as tab-delimited or comma-delimited text files, Excel lists, or Access databases. The data must be stored in a structured way that allows Word to distinguish one item of information from another and one set of items from another.

Records →

Fields →

Headers and field names →

In the table, each row, which is called a *record*, contains the set of variable items for one printout. You can include as many records as you want in a data source. Each cell (the intersection of a column and a row), which is called a *field*, contains one variable item. The number of fields you can have is practically unlimited. The first record (the top row of the table) is called the *header*. Each field in the header contains a *field name* that identifies the contents of the column below it.

As you'll see later in the chapter, the result of merging the sample main document and data source shown on the previous page is three letters, each with their appropriate information instead of the merge fields. Some mail merge documents are pretty complex and can include conditional elements, mathematical calculations, logical comparisons, or branching instructions. But most are as simple as the sample documents you'll use in this chapter.

In addition to creating letters, mail merge is a handy tool for filling in forms, and it is particularly useful when the information needed to fill in the forms is already included in a database or spreadsheet. For example, you might use mail merge to print invoices, checks, and insurance forms, as well as all kinds of labels—for mailings and for collections of disks, audio cassettes, CDs, video tapes, and books. Printing labels of various types is such a common use of mail merge that Word includes instructions to guide you through the process. We'll have a look at labels later. Right now, let's create the sample form letter.

Creating Simple Form Letters

Field location

The order of the fields in the data source is not important to the operation of the mail merge feature. The main document can use any combination of fields in any order. If the order of the data source fields is significant, you can insert them manually wherever you want or move them after they have been inserted.

The first stage of creating a form letter is to take a few moments to plan it. You might draft a sample letter and mark all the words or phrases that will vary from letter to letter. Then you might organize your sources of information to make sure you have easy access to all the names, addresses, and other tidbits of information required. Only after these tasks have been completed will you actually create the main document and data source. Assume that you have already taken care of this planning stage so that you can now start the interesting part.

Creating the Main Document

Word walks you through the steps for creating four types of main documents: form letters, mailing labels, envelopes, and catalogs. (See page 164 for information about setting up labels, and see the tip on page 160 for a brief discussion of catalogs.) Let's get started on setting up your main document. Follow these steps:

1. After starting Word, choose New from the File menu and double-click the icon for the Letterhead template you created in Chapter 5.

2. Click the Save button. In the Save As dialog box, assign the name *Main Document 1* to the document, and save it in the My Documents folder.

3. Choose Mail Merge from the Tools menu to display the dialog box shown here:

← Starting mail merge

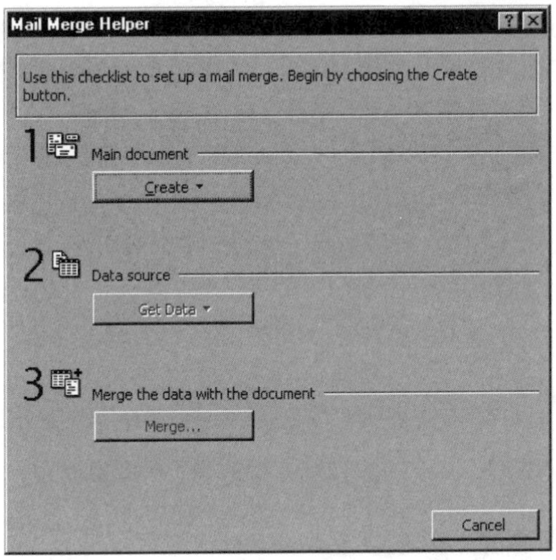

As you can see, Word is ready to lead you through the mail merge process.

4. Follow the suggestion at the top of the dialog box and click the Create button. A list drops down, offering you the choices shown on the next page.

Creating a new main document

You don't have to create the main document before you begin the mail merge operation. After selecting Form Letters from the Create list in the Mail Merge Helper dialog box (see the next page), simply click New Main Document to open a new document and add an Edit button to the dialog box. You can then use the Edit button to switch to the main document at any time and type or edit it.

Specifying the main
document type

5. Select Form Letters. Word displays this dialog box:

6. Click the Active Window button to use Main Document 1 as your main document.

Now let's create the data source, which will contain all the variable information for the form letters.

Creating the Data Source

With most word processors, the data source has to exist before you begin the mail merge process. With Word, you can either open an existing data source or you can have Word guide you through the procedure for creating one, like this:

1. With the Mail Merge Helper dialog box still open, click the Get Data button to drop down this list of options:

Data source preparation

Before creating the data source for a mail merge document, you should think through how the data source will be used. If you plan on sorting any of your data (see the tip on page 162), you need to put the information you want to sort in separate fields. If you think you may use the data source for several kinds of mail merge documents, you may want to add extra fields that won't be used in one type of document but will in another. For example, in an address label document, you may want to include a name and job title, such as *Al Pine, President*, but in the salutation of a letter, you may only want to include the first or last name (*Dear Mr. Pine:* or *Dear Al:*). You'll have more flexibility if you include all the information but organize it in separate fields.

2. Select Create Data Source to display this dialog box, which helps set up the fields of the data source:

Setting up a new data source

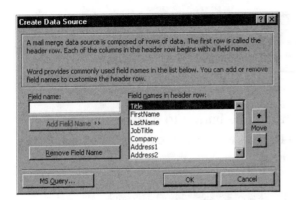

3. The list box on the right displays commonly used field names. You want this data source to have FirstName, LastName, Company, Address, City, State, and PostalCode (zip) fields. You don't want the selected field name, Title, so click Remove Field Name to delete it from the list. Also remove JobTitle, Address2, Country, HomePhone, and WorkPhone.

Removing field names

4. Now remove Address1 from the list. With Address1 displayed in the Field Name edit box, delete the 1 and then click Add Field Name to add Address back to the list.

Editing field names

5. With Address still selected, click the Move Up arrow repeatedly to move the Address field up until it appears between Company and City. The dialog box now looks like this:

Rearranging field names

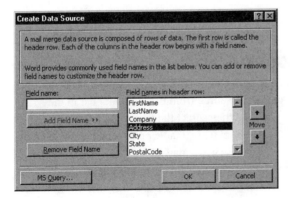

6. Click OK to close the dialog box. Word displays the Save As dialog box so that you can name the new data source.

Field name rules

Field names can have as many as 40 characters and can include letters, numbers, and underscore characters. Each field name must start with a letter and cannot contain spaces. To get around the "no spaces" rule, you can assign names such as LastName or Last_Name to multi-word fields.

7. Assign the name *Data Document 1* to the document, and click Save. Word displays this dialog box:

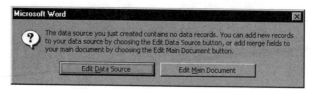

Entering records in the
data source

8. Click the Edit Data Source button to display the Data Form dialog box shown below, where you can begin entering records in the data source:

9. Go ahead and enter the information shown in the table on the facing page, pressing either Tab or Enter to move from field to field. After you fill in the last field in one record, click the Add New button or press Enter to move to a new record. You can use the arrows at the bottom of the screen to move back and forth through the records.

Adding a new record

Using an address book

When creating a mail merge letter or a set of labels (see page 164), you can use addresses entered in an electronic address book, such as Microsoft Outlook's contacts list. (See the tip on page 64.) Select Use Address Book from the Get Data list in the Mail Merge Helper dialog box. Then choose the address book you want to use and click OK.

Using an existing data source

If you want to use an existing Word document as the data source for your form letters, select Open Data Source from the Get Data list in the Mail Merge Helper dialog box, and then select the file you want to use. (The information in the file must be set up in a table or be separated by tabs or commas for Word to be able to use it as a mail merge data source.) You can also use existing database information from other applications as the data source. Candidates are databases created in certain versions of Microsoft Access, Microsoft Excel, Microsoft FoxPro, and dBASE. The process for opening a database created in another application is basically the same as that for opening a Word document, although a file conversion program (supplied with Word) is often needed to complete the task.

Field	Record1	Record2	Record3
FirstName	*Tim*	*Pete*	*Brooke*
LastName	*Buhr*	*Moss*	*Trout*
Company		*Mt. Meany Expeditions*	*The Great Outdoors Inc.*
Address	*947 St. Clair Road*	*14 River St.*	*1432 West Colorado Hwy.*
City	*Conway*	*Duckabush*	*Colorado Springs*
State	*NH*	*WA*	*CO*
PostalCode	*03818*	*98311*	*80901*

10. After entering the three records, click OK. Word closes the dialog box and returns to the main document.

Completing the Main Document

When you return to the main document, the most obvious change is that the Mail Merge toolbar has joined the Standard and Formatting toolbars at the top of the screen. This toolbar makes it easy to add placeholders for the variable information that will be merged from the data source. You might want to move the pointer over its buttons to orient yourself.

The Mail Merge toolbar

The next task is to type the text of the letter, inserting merge field placeholders. Let's start by entering the addressee information, which consists almost entirely of merge fields:

1. Press Ctrl+End to move to the blank paragraph below the letterhead. Press Enter and then format the new blank paragraph as left-aligned, 12-point, regular Times New Roman.

2. Click the Insert Merge Field button on the Mail Merge toolbar to drop down a list of the available fields.

Inserting a merge field

3. Click FirstName. The FirstName merge field appears at the insertion point, enclosed in chevrons. (If Word displays {MERGEFIELD FirstName} instead of <<FirstName>>, press Alt+F9 to turn off the display of codes and turn on the display of merge fields. If Word displays the first name from the first record in the data source, click the View Merged Data button on the Mail Merge toolbar to toggle it off and display the merge field.)

4. Press the Spacebar, click the Insert Merge Field button again, click LastName to insert that merge field, and press Enter to start a new line. Repeat this procedure for the Company merge field and the Address merge field.

5. Click Insert Merge Field, insert City, type a comma and a space, insert State, type a space, and insert PostalCode.

6. Press Enter a couple of times, and then type *Dear* and a space.

7. Insert the FirstName merge field, type a colon (:), and press Enter twice.

8. Now type the body of the letter, as shown here (we've magnified the screen for readability):

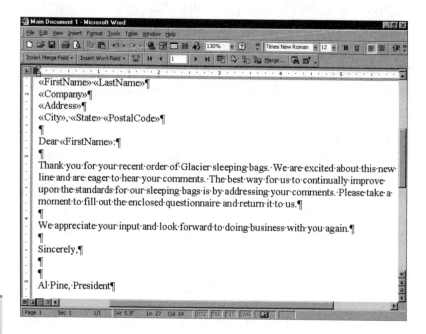

9. Save the document.

Merging the Documents

You are now ready to merge the main document with the data source. You have several options here. Notice the set of four buttons toward the right end of the Mail Merge toolbar. If you click the Check For Errors button, Word will ascertain whether the main document and data source are correctly set up. If you click the Merge To New Document button, Word merges the main document with the data source and puts the resulting letters in a new document that you can save and print later. If you click the Merge To Printer button, Word merges the main document and data source but sends them directly to the printer. If you click the Merge button, Word displays a dialog box in which you can specify where to merge the records, which records to merge, whether blank fields are to be printed, and so on. Let's experiment:

1. Click the Check For Errors button to display these options:

2. Select the Simulate option and click OK. If you followed our instructions, you'll see a dialog box announcing that Word found no mail merge errors. (If there are any errors, Word points them out so that you can correct them.) Click OK to return to your document.

3. Now click the Merge To New Document button. Word opens a new document window called *Form Letters1* and then "prints" the letters to the document, with a section break between each letter, like this:

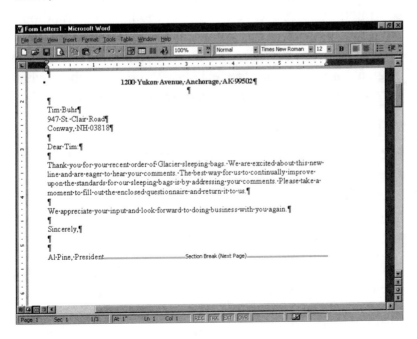

The Check For Errors button

The Merge To New Document button

Merging selected records

If your data source contains many records and you want to merge only those records that meet certain criteria (for example, only those with specific zip codes), you can "filter" the records to extract the ones you want. The filtering process is too complex to discuss thoroughly here, but briefly, you click the Query Options button in the Mail Merge Helper dialog box and specify your criteria on the Filter Records tab. For example, setting PostalCode equal to 98052 filters out for merging all the records in the data source with 98052 in the PostalCode field.

The Merge To Printer button

4. Close Form Letters1, saving it with the name *Form Letters* when prompted.

5. If your printer is turned on and you want to try the Merge To Printer button, go ahead and click it, and then click OK in the Print dialog box. The printed letters will look similar to those shown at the beginning of the chapter.

Now that you know how to do simple mail merges, let's look at some more sophisticated mail merge capabilities.

Creating More Sophisticated Letters

You named the main document and data source for this example Main Document 1 and Data Document 1, respectively, but you could have saved them with any valid names. And you can open and edit the documents just like any other documents. The data source is just a normal document that contains a table, so you can add fields and records to this table the same way you can add columns and rows to any table. And you can add tables, graphs, pictures, and various types of Word fields to the main document. You can even include fields that cause the mail merge process to pause and prompt for additional information that is not included in the data source.

Word gives you several methods of controlling exactly what is printed in a merged document. Although these methods are not very complicated, a complete explanation of them is beyond the scope of this book. However, let's quickly turn the original form letter into one that makes a decision about what to print, just to give you an idea of what can be done.

Adding Fields to the Data Source

Let's create a letter thanking people for their order of Glacier sleeping bags, and include a paragraph that Word will print only if the order is over a certain amount. To allow Word to make the printing decision, you have to add a field to the data source to hold the amount of the order. Follow these steps:

1. Because Data Document 1 is just another Word document, open the file as usual to display it in a window on top of the main document.

Catalogs

When you want to create lists of information using the fields in a data source, select the Catalog option from the main document's Create list in the Mail Merge Helper dialog box. For example, suppose your company wants to create a list of employee names and emergency phone numbers using three fields from a personnel database. After selecting Catalog and identifying the data source, you enter the LastName, FirstName, and EmergencyPhone fields just once in the main document. (Be sure to press Enter after the last field.) When you click the Merge To New Document button on the Mail Merge toolbar, Word creates one document containing the specified information for all the employees in the data source.

2. If opening the data source doesn't display the Database tool-bar, right-click one of the existing toolbars and choose Database from the shortcut menu. If you don't see gridlines, choose Show Gridlines from the Table menu.

3. Click the Manage Fields button on the Database toolbar to display this dialog box:

The Manage Fields button

4. Type *Order* in the Field Name edit box and press Enter. Word adds the field to the bottom of the list and to the right end of the table. Click OK to close the dialog box.

5. Click an insertion point in the first cell of the Order column and type *250*. Press the Down Arrow key, type *600*, press the Down Arrow key, and type *1250*.

6. Click the Save button and then click the Mail Merge Main Document button on the Database toolbar to activate the open main document.

The Mail Merge Main Document button

Editing the Main Document

Instead of creating a new main document from scratch, let's edit the one you've already saved. Here's how:

1. Click an insertion point to the left of the *W* in the second sentence of the letter (the one that begins *We are excited*).

2. Type *Your order of $*.

3. Click the Insert Merge Field button and select the new Order field. Then type a space followed by *worth of merchandise is greatly appreciated.*

Adding data to the data source

After creating a new field in the data source, you can add the field information in two ways. You can type the information directly in the data source table; or you can click the Edit Data Source button on the Database toolbar to display its dialog box, where you can add the field information to each record in turn.

4. With the insertion point still to the left of the *W* in *We are excited*, press the Spacebar and then press Enter twice, leaving a space after the sentence you just typed.

Next you need to enter the conditional statement that will control printing of an additional sentence based on the amount of the contribution. Follow these steps:

Inserting a conditional statement →

1. Click an insertion point after the space at the end of the new sentence, click the Insert Word Field button to drop down a list of fields, and select the If...Then...Else... option. Word displays this dialog box:

Sorting data

In some circumstances, you may want to sort the information contained in your data source before the merge operation. For example, to print letters in last-name alphabetical order or labels in zip code order, select the appropriate column in the data source document and click the Sort Ascending button on the Database toolbar. For the more complex sorts—those that use more than one sort criteria—choose Sort from the Table menu and select the appropriate options. During the mail merge process, you can click the Query Options button and set up your sort criteria on the Sort Records tab of the Query Options dialog box.

2. Click the arrow to the right of the Field Name edit box to drop down a list of field names. Scroll down to Order and click it to insert it in the Field Name edit box.

3. Drop down the Comparison list and select Greater Than.

4. Click the Compare To edit box and type *500*.

5. Press Tab to move to the Insert This Text box, and type the following:

Because of the size of your order, we are offering you an additional 10% off on your next purchase.

If the result of the conditional statement is true—that is, if the value of the order is greater than $500—Word will enter this text in the merged document.

6. Leave the Otherwise Insert This Text box blank, because you don't want Word to print anything if the conditional statement is not true—that is, if the value of the order is $500 or less.

7. Click OK to close the dialog box, and then press Alt+F9 to turn off the display of merge fields and turn on the display of field codes, which look like this:

Displaying field codes

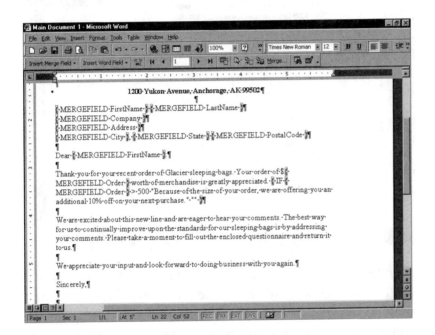

8. Press Alt+F9 again to turn off the display of field codes, and then save the main document as *Main Document 2*.

That's all there is to it. You now have several ways to check the results of your efforts. You can click one of the buttons on the Mail Merge toolbar to merge the letters to a document or to the printer, or you can look at the results right in the main document. Try this:

1. Click the View Merged Data button on the Mail Merge toolbar to display the data from the first record in place of the merge fields.

The View Merged Data button

2. Click the right and left arrows on the Mail Merge toolbar to cycle through the records in your data source. (The current

Cycling through records

record number is displayed in the box between the arrows.) The merged data for the third record, which has an order of $1,250, is shown here:

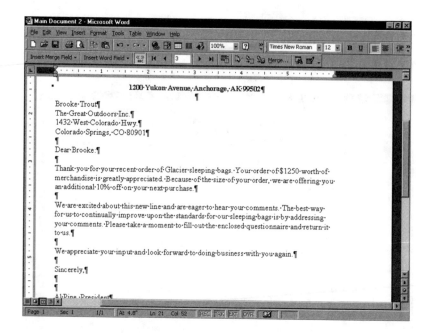

3. If you entered orders of $250, $600, and $1,250 for the three customers, the first customer's letter doesn't have the extra sentence and the second and third letters do. Try changing the comparison operator from > to < (less than) by pressing Alt+F9 to display the field codes, selecting the > symbol, and typing a < in its place. Then press Alt+F9 again and cycle through the records to see the result.

Changing the comparison operator

4. If you want, merge the letters to a document, save it as *Letters*, and then save and close all open documents to prepare for the next example.

Now let's take a look at how the mail merge feature can help you print labels.

Creating Labels

When you used the Mail Merge Helper dialog box to create a form letter, you undoubtedly noticed that it could also be used to create labels and envelopes. In this section, we discuss the procedure for printing multiple labels. (If you want to print just one label or envelope, use the Envelopes And Labels command on the Tools menu, as described in the tip below.) The procedure for printing multiple envelopes is similar to the one we'll describe here; if anything, you'll find that printing envelopes is easier because you have fewer options to deal with.

Follow the steps below to create a set of mailing labels for the sample form letter using the data source you created earlier. (To create other labels, you will first need to set up and save a data source so that you can select it in step 4; see page 154.)

1. Click the New button on the toolbar to create a new document that you can use as the main document for your labels.

2. Choose Mail Merge from the Tools menu to display the Mail Merge Helper dialog box shown earlier on page 153.

3. Click the Create button in the Main Document section and select Mailing Labels from the list of options. When Word asks whether you want to use the active window or create a new document, click Active Window.

4. Back in the Mail Merge Helper dialog box, click the Get Data button in the Data Source section. Select Open Data Source from the list of options, and double-click Data Document 1, the source document you created earlier.

5. Word advises that you now need to create the main document. Click Set Up Main Document to display the dialog box shown below, which helps you define the label you want to use:

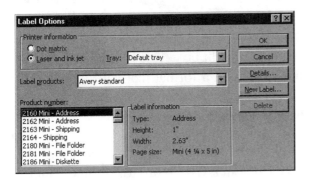

One envelope or label

If you want to print a single envelope or label, choose Envelopes And Labels from the Tools menu. You can then click the tab for either Envelopes or Labels in the resulting dialog box. Click Options to change the envelope or label size and click OK. Enter the information you want to appear on the envelope or label and click Print. Or click Add To Document to view the envelope or New Document to view the label on the screen before you print.

Notice that you can select either Dot Matrix or Laser And Ink Jet in the Printer Information section. This setting determines the type of labels displayed in the Product Number list. Laser or ink jet labels typically come on 8½-by-11-inch sheets, and dot matrix labels come on fanfold paper.

Displaying information about a label

6. Scroll through the Product Number list to get an idea of what is available. (You can highlight an item to see general information about it in the adjacent Label Information section. Click the Details button to see more information about the selected label.)

7. Select the 5161 Address label if you have a laser printer or the 4143 Address label if you have a dot matrix printer. Click Details. This dialog box appears for the 5161 Address label:

As you can see, the Information dialog box displays a drawing of the selected label, with its characteristics listed below. You can change each characteristic—margins, pitch, height, width, and number across and down—by entering a new value in the corresponding edit box. This flexibility is handy if you want to print labels in a format that isn't included in Word's lists. You can select a format that is similar and then fine-tune it in the Information dialog box.

Other types of labels

In addition to regular address labels, Word can print labels for packages, file folders, name tags, disks, audio and video tapes, and several types of cards. It is worth checking whether Word can help automate some of your routine label-making tasks.

8. Try changing the characteristics of this label, and watch the drawing change. (If you click OK, Word asks you to enter a

name for your custom label in the Label Name edit box.) Then click Cancel to close the dialog box without recording your changes.

9. Click OK to close the Label Options dialog box. Word displays this dialog box so that you can create the label format for your main document:

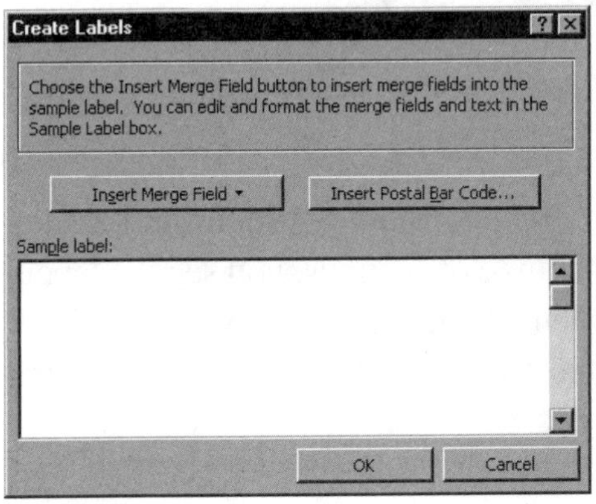

10. Next create the label format the same way you created the addressee portion of the form letter earlier in the chapter. Click the Insert Merge Field button, select FirstName, press the Spacebar, click Insert Merge Field, select LastName, and press Enter. Then insert the Company, Address, City, State, and PostalCode merge fields, like this:

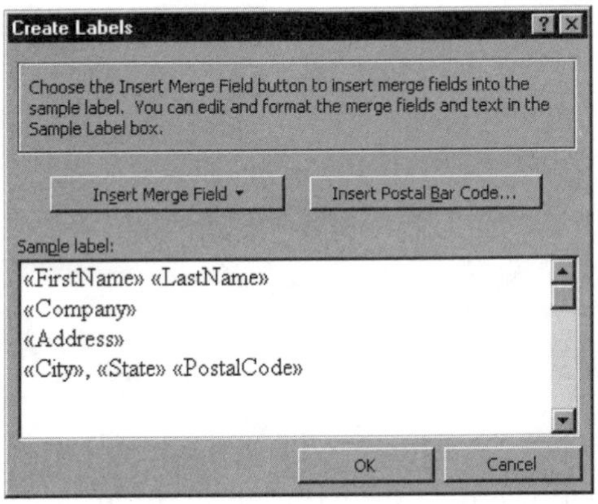

Inserting merge fields in a label

Be sure the bottom line of the label text consists of the three merge fields shown above, with punctuation and spacing included.

Adding bar codes

You can cut down on postage costs for bulk mailings by printing a POSTNET bar code on your labels or envelopes. To insert a bar code, click the Insert Postal Bar Code button in the Create Labels (or Envelope Address) dialog box, select the fields that contain the zip code and street address (or post office box number), and click OK. Word prints the bar code at the top of the label (or above the address on an envelope).

11. Click OK to return to the Mail Merge Helper dialog box, and then click Merge in the Merge The Data With The Document section to display this dialog box:

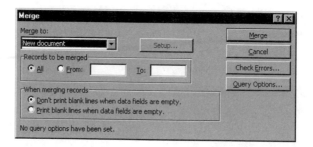

12. Click Merge to merge the labels to a new document rather than to the printer. After a couple of seconds, you see the labels shown below on your screen. (If necessary, choose the Show Gridlines command from the Table menu to display the margins of each label.)

An entire sheet of the same label

Sometimes you may need to print an entire sheet of the same label—for example, for your return address. Choose Envelopes And Labels from the Tools menu. Click the Labels tab and type the desired information on the label in the Address box. Click the Full Page Of The Same Label option in the Print section, then click Options and select the label style you are using, and click OK. Finally, click Print to send the sheet of labels directly to your printer, or click New Document to insert the label information in a document that you can format, edit, and save just like any other Word document.

If you want, save the merged document with a name such as *Labels* so that you can print it later. Save the main document with a name such as *Main Document Labels* so that you can reuse it in the future.

That's all there is to it. You should test-print the labels on plain paper to check their alignment, and then you can replace the paper with label sheets and print away! After you have been through the process once or twice, you will probably find that it takes you less time to merge a batch of labels than it did to read these instructions.

Printing a batch of envelopes is even easier than labels. With a new, blank document displayed on your screen, create a default return address for your envelopes by choosing Envelopes And Labels from the Tools menu, entering a return address in the Return Address box on the Envelopes tab, and clicking Add To Document. When Word asks if you want to save the return address as the default, click Yes. Next choose Mail Merge from the Tools menu. Select Envelopes from the list that drops down when you click the Create button in the Main Document section of the Mail Merge Helper dialog box, and follow Word's instructions for selecting a data source and setting up the main document in the active window. The first time you create envelopes after specifying the return address, Word warns that it will overwrite the return address displayed in the active document with the mail merge information you just set up. (This does not mean that Word will delete your default return address information.) Click OK and then click the Merge button to merge the envelopes to a new document or to your printer. When you use the Mail Merge command to create envelopes in the future, Word will automatically add the return address to the top left corner of your envelopes.

Printing envelopes

Congratulations! You have now completed your Quick Course in Word. By now you should feel comfortable with most aspects of the program. With the basics you have learned here, together with the Help feature and the sample documents that come with Word, you should be able to tackle the creation of some fairly sophisticated documents.

Index

Quick Course® Books

Offering beginning to intermediate training, Quick Course® books are updated regularly. For information about the most recent titles, call 1-800-854-3344 or e-mail us at quickcourse@otsiweb.com.

AVAILABLE QUICK COURSE®BOOKS		
1-58278-005-6	Quick Course® in Microsoft Access 2000	$14.95
1-879399-73-3	Quick Course® in Microsoft Access 97	$14.95
1-879399-52-0	Quick Course® in Microsoft Access 7	$14.95
1-879399-32-6	Quick Course® in Access 2	$14.95
1-58278-003-X	Quick Course® in Microsoft Excel 2000	$14.95
1-879399-71-7	Quick Course® in Microsoft Excel 97	$14.95
1-879399-51-2	Quick Course® in Microsoft Excel 7	$14.95
1-879399-28-8	Quick Course® in Excel 5	$14.95
1-58278-008-0	Quick Course® in Microsoft FrontPage 2000	$14.95
1-879399-91-1	Quick Course® in the Internet Using Microsoft Internet Explorer 5	$14.95
1-879399-68-7	Quick Course® in Microsoft Internet Explorer 4	$14.95
1-879399-67-9	Quick Course® in the Internet Using Netscape Navigator, ver. 2 & 3	$14.95
1-58278-001-3	Quick Course® in Microsoft Office 2000	$24.95
1-879399-69-5	Quick Course® in Microsoft Office 97	$24.95
1-879399-54-7	Quick Course® in Microsoft Office for Windows 95/NT	$24.95
1-879399-39-3	Quick Course® in Microsoft Office for Windows, ver. 4.3	$24.95
1-58278-006-4	Quick Course® in Microsoft Outlook 2000	$14.95
1-879399-80-6	Quick Course® in Microsoft Outlook 98	$14.95
1-58278-004-8	Quick Course® in Microsoft PowerPoint 2000	$14.95
1-879399-72-5	Quick Course® in Microsoft PowerPoint 97	$14.95
1-879399-33-4	Quick Course® in PowerPoint 4	$14.95
1-58278-007-2	Quick Course® in Microsoft Publisher 2000	$14.95
1-58278-000-5	Quick Course® in Microsoft Windows 2000	$15.95
1-879399-81-4	Quick Course® in Microsoft Windows 98	$15.95
1-879399-34-2	Quick Course® in Windows 95	$14.95
1-879399-14-8	Quick Course® in Windows 3.1	$14.95
1-879399-22-9	Quick Course® in Windows for Workgroups	$14.95
1-879399-64-4	Quick Course® in Windows NT Workstation 4	$16.95

AVAILABLE QUICK COURSE®BOOKS		
1-58278-002-1	Quick Course® in Microsoft Word 2000	$14.95
1-879399-70-9	Quick Course® in Microsoft Word 97	$14.95
1-879399-50-4	Quick Course® in Microsoft Word 7	$14.95
1-879399-27-X	Quick Course® in Word 6	$14.95
1-879399-49-0	Quick Course® in WordPerfect 6.1 for Windows	$14.95

Volume discounts available for orders of 5 or more of the same title.

Quick Course® Workbooks

Providing additional practice exercises and true/false and fill-in-the-blank quizzes, the workbooks are sold only with an accompanying Quick Course® book and in quantities of FIVE or more. Exercise and answer files are provided in an Instructor's Resource packet, which is free with orders of TEN or more workbooks.

AVAILABLE WORKBOOKS		
1-879399-78-4	Microsoft Access 97 Workbook	$11.95
1-879399-84-9	Access 97 Instructor's Resource Packet	$11.95
1-879399-77-6	Microsoft Excel 97 Workbook	$11.95
1-879399-85-7	Excel 97 Instructor's Resource Packet	$11.95
1-58278-010-2	Microsoft Office 2000 Workbook	$14.95
1-58278-014-5	Office 2000 Instructor's Resource Packet	$14.95
1-879399-74-1	Microsoft Office 97 Workbook	$14.95
1-879399-83-0	Office 97 Instructor's Resource Packet	$14.95
1-879399-65-2	Microsoft Office 95 Workbook	$14.95
1-879399-66-0	Office 95 Instructor's Resource Packet	$14.95
1-879399-46-6	Microsoft Office ver. 4.3 Workbook	$14.95
1-879399-45-8	Office 4.3 Instructor's Resource Packet	$14.95
1-879399-79-2	Microsoft PowerPoint 97 Workbook	$11.95
1-879399-86-5	PowerPoint 97 Instructor's Resource Packet	$11.95
1-879399-76-8	Microsoft Word 97 Workbook	$11.95
1-879399-87-3	Word 97 Instructor's Resource Packet	$11.95
1-879399-88-1	Microsoft Windows 98 Workbook	$12.75
1-879399-89-X	Windows 98 Instructor's Resource Packet	$12.75

Prices and availability are subject to change without notice.

Quick Course® Online Training

For those times when books alone don't quite fit the bill, Quick Course® training is now offered online.

This exciting new CD-ROM-based, interactive option incorporates video demonstrations into the acclaimed Quick Course® hands-on training format. Each title is fully searchable and includes a detailed table of contents and a comprehensive index. Document files are provided for each unit so that tasks can be tackled in the order presented in the course or on an as-needed basis. Web-based support is provided for all online courses.

Quick Course® online training can be delivered via CD-ROM, the Internet, or an intranet. It is ideal for self-paced training and can facilitate and enhance instructor-led courses. Titles are sold as individual copies or as site licenses. Please call for pricing information.

AVAILABLE IN ONLINE FORMAT
Quick Course® in Microsoft Access 2000
Quick Course® in Microsoft Excel 2000
Quick Course® in Microsoft FrontPage 2000
Quick Course® in Microsoft Office 2000
Quick Course® in Microsoft PowerPoint 2000
Quick Course® in Microsoft Publisher 2000
Quick Course® in Microsoft Word 2000